Caring for your Rescue Dog

by Louisa Adams

angelapatchellbooks

Published by Angela Patchell Books Ltd
www.angelapatchellbooks.com

registered address
36 Victoria Road, Dartmouth
Devon, TQ6 9SB

contact sales and editorial
sales@angelapatchellbooks.com or
angie@angelapatchellbooks.com

copyright APB 2008

All rights reserved. No part of this publication maybe reproduced, stored in a retrieval system or transmitted in any form or by any means, electronic, mechanical, photocopying, downloaded, recordings or otherwise, without the permission of the copyright holder.

ISBN: 978-1-906245-02-3

book concept by Angie Patchell

book design by Toby Mathews

printed by SNP Corporation

Caring for your Rescue Dog

by Louisa Adams

Contents

Foreword

Introduction – Finding Your Perfect Rescue Dog

1. Understanding Your Rescue Dog   p 10
6 most common behavioural problems and how to overcome them
1. Scared dogs
2. Emotionally stressed
3. Barking excessively
4. Aggression with other dogs and people
5. Breed Temperaments
6. Destructive – being left alone

2. Caring for a Rescue Dog   p 18
5 tips to caring for your rescue dog
1. Your dog's health
2. A balanced diet
3. Exercise and mental stimulation
4. Training
5. Travelling with your dog

3. 60 Dog Rescue Stories   p 27

… The last word

Foreword

"I was going to write a foreword for this book when out of the blue, a lady who had already contributed a story sent me the following. Thank you Von Barber for writing such a heartfelt Dog Rescue Mission Statement. I think her words reflect the views of the many contributors that have made this book possible."
(Louisa Adams)

Why I rescue dogs …

Every one is born in this life with a purpose, unfortunately most of us go through life never knowing or understanding why we are here. I was one of those people until the day I adopted my first special needs dog, a pure white deaf boxer we named Doofy. I was so amazed by him and the challenges we faced that I started doing some research into deaf dogs. I found out that in most cases dogs that are born deaf are killed at birth, this was not an option that sat right with me knowing how much joy Doofy was giving us. I couldn't understand why being born deaf was a certain death sentence considering that these dogs can lead normal, happy, healthy lives with a few minor considerations. So from that day I decided to keep an eye out for any deaf dogs that may need new homes and to rescue them and find the right owners that would appreciate the gift of sharing a life with a deaf dog could bring.

It wasn't long before I found that it wasn't only the deaf dogs that were considered a waste of time to re-home. there were the blind, the old, the ones with abuse issues, the ones considered all to hard and the not so easy to re-home and the overwhelming need to help and save these dogs was my calling and Victorian Canine Rescue was born.

I am often asked why do you do rescue, why even bother, my answer to the people asking is this.

"If I was given the option of a million dollars or a damaged unwanted dog which would I take; the answer is simple although not understood by most, I would take the damaged unwanted dog; to be given the gift of working with this dog … to have a dog so damaged that it has given up the will to live, and all trust in humans, to have their spirit so damaged that everyone else thinks they are beyond help, to see the dog want to be touched and not to cower down, to treat the dog with kindness and respect not like a piece of trash that can just be disposed of when they are no longer wanted. The first glimmer of trust in the dogs eye, the first wag of its tail, and nudge of its nose under your hand the first time you feel that they trust in what you are doing to help them no amount of money can buy."

I believe I do make a difference to that one dog; the dog that no-one else could be bothered with. I gave it a chance to have a new life and in return it gave me the memory of that first tail wag, the first loving, trusting look, and the drive to save another one. That is why I do rescue.

Von Barber
Victorian Canine Rescue

Introduction

Finding your perfect rescue dog

There are many open avenues to potential adopters – private rescue, local dog pounds, city shelters and the Internet. The thousands of available dogs is the easy part but …

Before you start looking:

- How big is your space – do you have a garden? Most rescue centres will not let you adopt a dog without outside space. If you rent, any worthwhile rescue home will verify with your landlord to check dogs are allowed.

- Is your house and garden secured?

- Are you willing to pay for (possibly) large vets' bills and ongoing expenses such as vaccinations?

- As a family discuss behaviour parameters and agree on them before allowing a dog in the house. It's no good one person allowing the dog on the couch if the other chastises it.

- What breed of dog best suits your situation? Do you really want a pedigree? Remember that mixed breed dogs tend not to have so many health issues as purebreds – they have a stronger genetic code. If you must have a pedigree, DO NOT BUY from a puppy farm! Do a thorough background check on the breeder even if they are registered.

- Remember that adopting from a rescue home usually means that the dog will be vaccinated, often neutered, or spayed and the shelter should have information of the dog's history – it may not be a pleasant history but this will help you to make the right choice.

- Think about adopting an older dog. Depending on the dog's history, this usually negates the house training issue, the dog may understand basic commands, and in general, they are likely to be better behaved than a puppy. Put yourself in an older dog's position – there are hundreds of older dogs up for adoption because their callous owners replaced them with a "cute" puppy.

The paperwork process

What to expect at the rescue centre:
The rules for allowing people to adopt a dog vary. If the shelter or rescue home asks no questions, then ask yourself if you should be adopting from them. However, generally speaking the paperwork will ask for the following:

- Personal information – address, phone etc.
- Evidence of house ownership or a written authorization to allow dogs (including maximum weight of dog) from a landlord.
- If you have previously owned a dog.
- Your vet's address.
- Is someone home during the day?
- Have you ever surrendered an animal to the pound or shelter?
- Information about your children and other pets.
- If the dog is not already sterilised, it is usually a condition of adoption that you will get the dog fixed and bring in the paperwork from the vet.

There are numerous other questions that you may be asked depending on the shelter, but a few things to take into consideration are:

- Take all family members with you when looking for a dog at a shelter or pound – everyone needs to be in agreement.
- Do you have a pool – if so, is the cover secure so that the dog cannot wriggle underneath it?
- Check with the shelter if the dog has been vaccinated and make sure you pick up the relevant paperwork – the same applies if the dog has been sterilized.
- Is the dog negative for heartworm and parvo virus? Has the dog been wormed? Read up on these issues before adopting.

Understanding Your Rescue Dog

6 most common behavioural problems and how to overcome them ...

1. Scared dogs
2. Emotionally stressed
3. Barking excessively
4. Aggression with other dogs and people
5. Breed temperaments
6. Destructive – being left alone

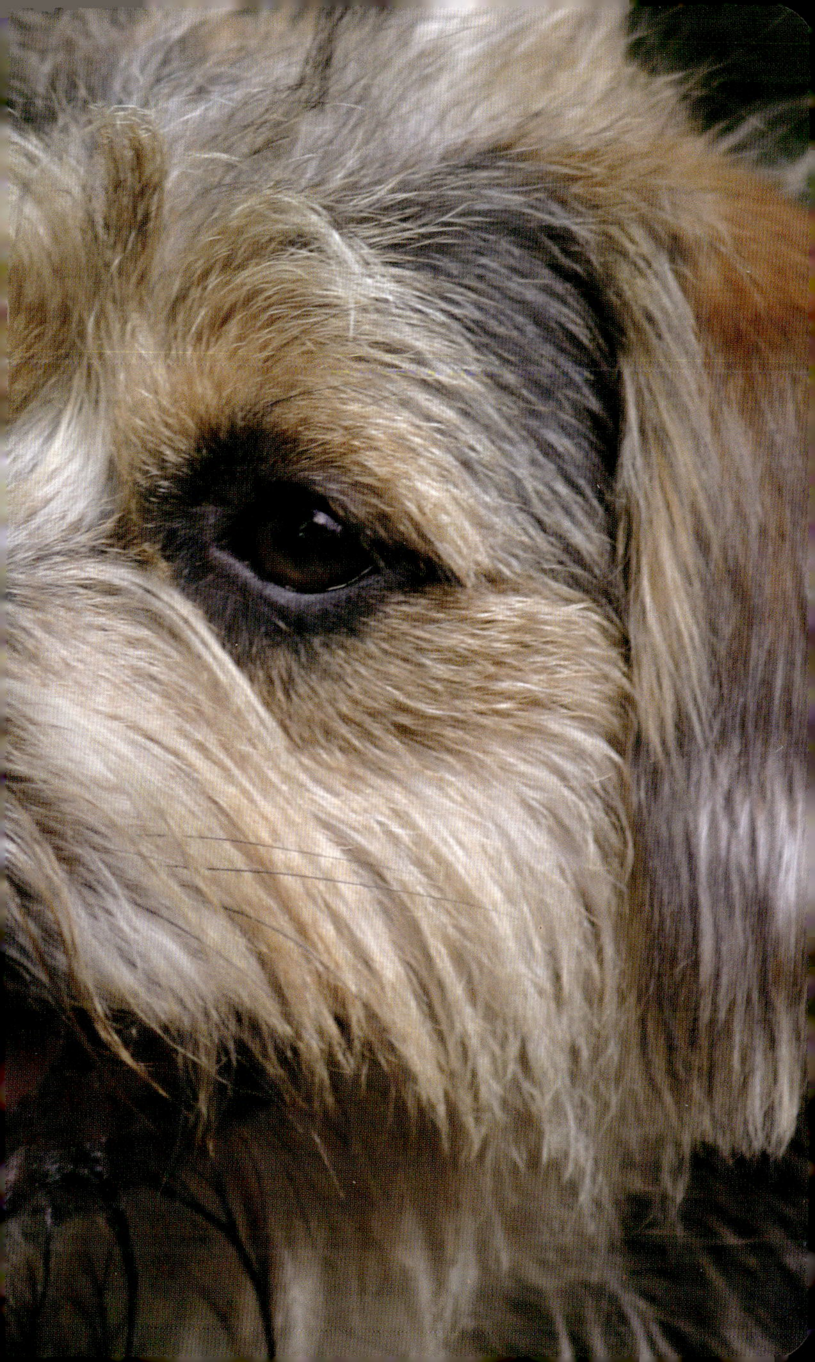

Scared dogs

When dogs are scared they may hide, run, cower, show aggressiveness, consistently lick their nose, shake, and bark. Naturally, an abused dog may well exhibit scared behaviour which may rectify itself as the dog gains trust. Here are a few suggestions:

- If your dog is scared of a specific object, don't hide the object. Leave it out and move it around until your dog becomes used to it.
- Give your dog time to investigate people or items that cause fear. Dogs react better to high toned voices. People often tell me that their dog is scared of men but it is often the deeper tone of voice that they associate with punishment.
- Don't leave your dog in the room with a stranger.
- Use music in the car and house to get the dog used to noise.
- If your dog is scared of other dogs, gradual socializing usually helps but depending on a dog's history, some dogs will always be happier as the sole pet.
- Above all, give your dog time to re-adjust to new situations.
- Don't let strange children pet your dog if it is nervous. Explain to the child that you would prefer them not to touch your dog.

Emotionally stressed

Your dog's history will naturally play an important part in how you approach the first few weeks. Ask the rescue home for suggestions, if your dog is undergoing treatment or needs medication, talk to your vet before bringing the dog home so you are prepared. You need to understand or at least try to predict your dog's emotional needs. Badly abused dogs are often not good with children or other dogs but again, a good rescue home/shelter will not allow the wrong dog to go to the wrong home. In any case, patience and trust are the essence. On the evidence of some of the stories in the book, it can take months of love and understanding before an emotionally stressed dog can even begin to feel secure and reciprocate its new found trust.

Any new environment will be stressful for your new dog regardless of its history. Get the bed, toys, blankets etc organized before you bring your dog home. Don't overwhelm your dog. For the first few days, keep your dog in a relatively confined area. By this I mean that if he is allowed to roam all over the house, it may be too much to absorb. Introduce your dog to each family member and to his outside space.

Once you have your dog, do not forget to get your dog identified – microchipped (mandatory in some countries) tattooed or, at the very least, a collar with an ID tag.

Barking excessively

A dog that never stops barking is a nightmare to all concerned. Excessive barking can be caused by anxiety, attention seeking, boredom (very common indeed), over stimulation and some breeds simply bark more than others. Dogs may howl as an alternative to barking – also often caused by boredom, but with some breeds this is a form of communication. Dogs may also imitate sirens and certain sounds on the TV by howling. Training manuals recommend the following steps:

- Desensitize your dog to the sounds that cause the barking. There are various methods of doing this, usually by creating another distracting noise that takes the dog's mind of the issue. Read your training manual to find a method that works.
- Teach the dog the basic sit and be quiet command so you can use this immediately the dog barks. Reward the dog when he is sitting and quiet.
- Don't distract a barking dog with treats, yanking on its collar or picking it up.
- Adopt a calm stance – don't shout or smack the dog.
- Make sure your dog has toys to help counteract boredom. If a dog barks continually in the house or yard, it is usually because he's bored.

Aggression – with other dogs and people

Aggression towards people and other dogs usually stems from fear. This behaviour can also be reflected in over possessiveness towards toys and food. How aggressive your dog is depends on its breed and how your dog has been treated from birth. If your dog shows signs of aggression, it is imperative you seek expert help immediately, before the pattern becomes "imprinted" making the habit harder and harder to break.

Dogs are natural pack animals which form groups to protect their territory from other dogs. This is why not all dogs socialize well with strange dogs that are invited onto their ground. Dogs can develop fear of a myriad of things – from specific breeds, colours, noises, separation anxiety – the list of phobias is limitless.

As a dog owner, it is important that the dog feels safe within a specific space and that space is a calm haven for him to relax. Do not think that socializing your dog means inviting strange dogs to sniff him while he is on a lead. This is his time with you in control, and a strange dog while he is under your control will be seen as threatening. Let your dog play with others in an area where he feels safe and can use his natural body language to communicate to the other dogs.

If your dog becomes aggressive, check with the vet that he is not in some sort of pain. Be careful if you have dogs of different sizes as the smaller dog can be harmed even during a playful tussle. In a family with more than one dog, there will be an alpha dog. The alpha dog often exhibits more aggression in same sex packs, especially in non- sterilized dogs; another reason to get your dog fixed.

Naturally, with an adopted dog, it is critical that you find out as much as possible about the dog's history. If a dog's food or toys have been taken away as punishment, it is only natural he will become possessive and growl or even attack if this treatment has become habitual. I cannot stress enough the importance of dealing with aggression the minute it is exhibited. There are horror stories of animals attacking and killing animals and humans often because the owners have not recognized just how quickly this problem develops. This book does not have the scope to deal with this issue in depth so please seek expert advice.

Breed temperaments

Dogs are classified according to their breed and the following is a guide for each group. It is worth taking into account the type of breed (if known) of your rescue dog, even if they are cross breeds. Please remember that this is basic information only and to ask for specific breed traits at the time of adoption.

Terrier Group
Terriers love to dig – their natural instinct is to hunt underground for vermin but will also hunt larger animals such as rabbits and foxes. Their temperament is upbeat and bold, but they like to get their own way. While they are usually good with people and children, they need a firm hand and assertive training.

Gundog Group
This group comprises of Spaniels, Retrievers, Setters and Pointers. They were, and still are, bred to retrieve game. They are known for their good temperament, loving nature and are generally excellent with children. Because they are large, gundogs need copious amounts of exercise and should be trained as early as possible. They also require mental stimulation – toys, socializing etc. as they are easily bored.

Working Dog Group
Large and hardy this group makes the best "guard dog" and they are generally devoted to their owners. They are a courageous and intelligent group, with strong personalities to match their big hearts. Because this group has such powerful instincts, it is imperative that they have positive reinforcement at an early age as a maltreated working dog can turn what was a sweet natured animal into a large aggressor. Because of their size, they also need a lot of exercise and a firm hand.

Hound Group
The Hound Group is the largest of the groups and the breeds vary in size (from Afghan to Dachshund) and temperaments. Used for hunting, they are hardy and fast, and will need plenty of regular exercise. This group enjoys good health and a pleasant temperament. Their natural instinct is to hunt so obedience training is critical. The two types of hound are a gaze hound and a scent hound.

Pastoral or Herding Group
This group is often thought of as the classic Sheepdog as the breeds in this group are designed to herd. This instinct is innate and if you do not own a flock of sheep, you may well find yourself and your family herded into your kitchen! However, the Pastoral Group comprises of protective

and loving breeds, highly intelligent and anxious to obey commands. Because of their nature, they need constant stimulation and long walks.

Toy Group

Although small and affectionate, do not be fooled by their convenient size. Dogs in this group are highly demanding with strong, sometimes overbearing personalities and they need to know who is the boss. The benefits of this group are that they tend to need less exercise than bigger dogs and of course, eat less.

Utility Group

As the name implies, this diverse group was originally bred for practical purposes but they are now considered a non-sporting group. As the breeds in the Utility group are so very varied (Poodle, Akita, Dalmatian etc) if your rescue dog falls into this category, further research into the specific breed would be beneficial.

Destructive – being left alone

Dogs destroy things for various reasons and if you have a rescue dog with an abusive history, it may be fear or anger that is causing him to maul everything in sight. This may stop once the dog feels loved and secure but here are a couple of tips. If the behaviour continues it is best to consult a canine behavioural specialist about your dog's particular problem.

- Don't leave your dog for more that four hours at a time. If you cannot come home organize a dog walker or neighbour to help out.
- Make sure your dog has toys.
- Many experts advise leaving the radio or TV on for "company".
- It is natural for puppies to chew. Do not let your puppy have the run of the house but keep it in a comfortable but confined area with toys.
- Destructive dogs may have a surplus of energy which means their walks are too short.
- Destructive behaviour may also be caused by separation anxiety or a change in family dynamics – a new home, the death of a family member.
- Finally, don't punish your dog after the fact. Ignore bad Ignore bad behaviour and reinforce good behaviour with a treat or cuddle.

Caring for a Rescue Dog

5 tips for caring for your rescue dog

1. Your dog's health
2. A balanced diet
3. Excercise and mental stimulation
4. Training
5. Travelling with your dog

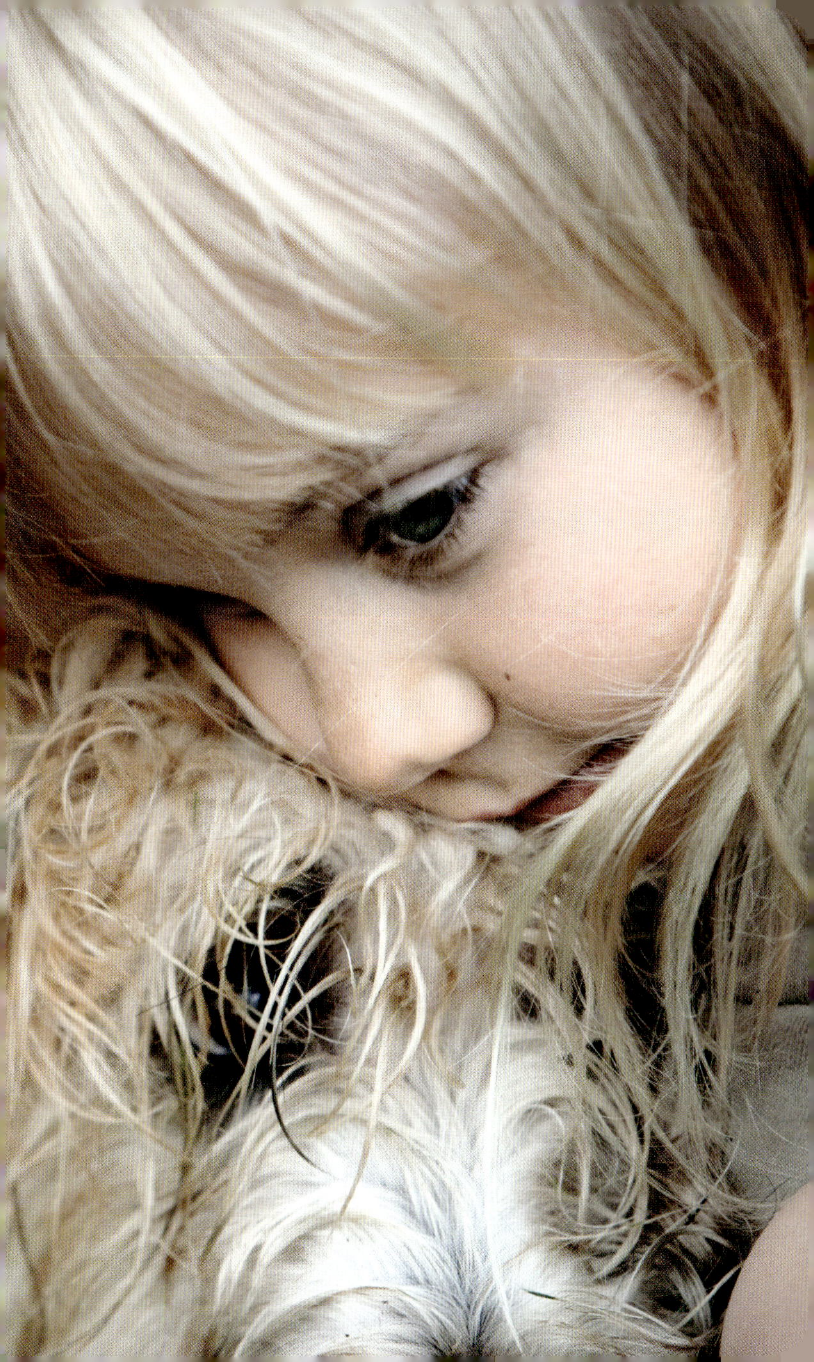

Your dog's health

If you adopt a dog with a known health problem, make sure you have done your research before your dog arrives in your home. Many older dogs have to take medication for various ailments and this issue should be discussed with the shelter and with your vet. If a dog needs tablets three times a day for example, are you around to make sure the pills are given on time. Messing around with a medication timetable can severely impair a drugs delivery system.

Many of the stories I received used homeopathic treatments on dogs with both health and emotional issues. Going the homeopathic route is a choice that your vet may acknowledge, but unless this is their field, he or she will not give alternative medicine or advice. Homeopathic medicine is often used as a compliment to traditional medicine.

Many people adopt dogs that have been abused and still have to have wound treatment or ongoing physiotherapy. If your dog has a wound in the process of healing, take this into account when you bring him home. Keep his area pristine, keep him away from other animals and in a quiet environment as stress is a known healing deterrent. He's going to have enough to cope with being in a strange home.

Above all, maintain a good relationship with your vet and follow the vet's instructions. If you are in any doubt about a vet's opinion, get a second one. Keeping your dog healthy is not so different to keeping yourself on top form.

A balanced diet

If you adopt a dog that requires a special diet, make sure that you have all the information up front and that you do not deviate from the dog's regime. Changing dog food brands, even if the label says for example "Light" for overweight dogs, can have disastrous effects. It is impossible to recommend a "healthy diet" that works for all dogs, however, in general, experts recommend a diet that consists of 55% protein and 14% carbohydrate. The balance should be in the form of healthy grains and vegetables.

Protein comes in the form of beef, rabbit, lamb, poultry, fish and eggs. Grains are usually in the form of barley and brown rice. Broccoli, peas, beans, dark green leafy vegetables plus orange vegetables like carrots or squash are full of antioxidants and are good for your dog in the same way they are good for human beings. They help counteract diseases like cancer and provide roughage for a healthy intestinal system.

There are many specially formulated dried dog foods available commercially and at the vet. These can range from special breed diets to dogs requiring a diet to counteract liver and urinary tract problems. Ask your vet which brand he advises for your dog and stick with it.

Other experts feel that a raw diet is the best method of delivering balanced nutrients. Many pet owners are under the misconception that feeding their dog raw produce and bones will expose their dogs to bacteria from meat or injuries from splintering bones. Bones only splinter once they have been cooked

– chicken bones being the worst and most dangerous culprits. Raw bones in fact, benefit both the digestive system and help maintain dogs' teeth.

Dogs love to eat grass for a reason. It helps them maintain the correct bacterial balance in their intestines. I understand that the odd spittle laden regurgitated grass on your best carpet can be annoying but never stop your dog from doing what is nature's way of keeping him healthy.

In general, keep your dog's diet as natural as possible. Supermarket dog food, especially canned, contain very high proportions of fat and sugar. Yes, it is cheaper but in the long run, the added cost of good food can counteract the cost of vet's fees down the line when your dog becomes ill from an unbalanced diet. Do not give your dog "human food". Feeding a dog scraps from the table encourages bad behaviour. There is nothing worse than a dog that hangs around the dining table begging all the time. Also, do not be tempted to empty leftovers into the dogs bowl however pleading his eyes might be at the time! There is nothing wrong with rewarding your dog's good behaviour with a dog treat, but make sure the treat is for dogs and that they are not given in handfuls or too often.

Exercise and mental stimulation

Unless you own a dog of the toy variety, running around in the back garden is not sufficient exercise. Insufficient exercise can result in severely debilitating diseases let alone obesity. A well-exercised dog is a happy dog. They sleep better, have more energy, and experience fewer socialization problems. From a health standpoint, they tend to live longer as exercise helps dogs build strong bones, muscles and improves the cardiovascular system. The new leash laws pose a problem if you live in a suburban area which means that walking your dog takes planning. Many places now have special dog parks which are great for socializing your dog but are still limiting. Throwing a ball a few times is not enough.

Naturally, the amount of exercise per day depends on the breed but generally, dogs need two good walks a day. They like routine, so even in bad weather, try and stick to a plan. Unless your dog is a working breed – on a farm for example – you need to find space where your dog can be off a lead and can do all the doggie things he likes without constraint. Walk your dog before feeding him. Build up your dog's stamina slowly, especially if he's a puppy or has had a traumatic past existence.

Experts advise that are wrong ways to exercise your dog. Anything that involves dragging a dog along on a lead at a fast pace is negligent – for example if you are on a bike or roller blading, don't think that this is a time cutting method to exercise your dog. I have even seen people exercising their dog with a leash from their car or worse still, encouraging the dog to run after the car. How lazy is that! If you want to jog with your dog, and he is of an appropriate breed, that's fine as long as he is safe. Make sure, like you, he has a chance to cool down and also that dogs like natural sniffing and toilet stops which, if you are on a specific timetable, may find frustrating.

Training

Proper training is essential for all dogs. If your dog has never had any former training and is not a puppy, it may be best to take him to certified training classes. Ask around for a dog trainer recommendation then ask the teacher for their credentials and methods of correction. Watch a class before taking your dog so you feel comfortable that this is the right person for your dog. Your vet or shelter should be able to advise you on this matter. If you plan to train your dog yourself, make sure you have clear, consistent, and realistic goals and stick to them. Certain breeds of dog have special behavioural traits so again, do your research beforehand so you don't have any surprises once your dog is at home. Destructive behaviour, avoidance and aggression are often signs of fear and anxiety. If you have adopted a dog with a sad past, expect to address these issues and have a concrete plan bearing in mind that altering negative behaviour takes time. Make sure all family members, especially children are on the same page so training is consistent and the dog does not receive mixed messages. Here are just a few book recommendations on training your dog:

Understanding the Rescue Dog by Carol Price

Dog Behavior and Training, Veterinary Advice for Owners by Lowell Ackerman

How to Teach A New Dog Old Tricks by Ian Dunbar

Don't Shoot the Dog! by Karen Pryor

RSPCA New Complete Dog Training Manual by Bruce Fogle

The Everything Dog Training and Tricks Book by Bielakiewicz, Brown & Shea.

Travelling with your dog

- Dogs suffer from motion sickness just like humans. Start by introducing your dog to the car and letting him sit in it without moving. Continue with short trips that end at one of his favourite places – the park or beach. The worst thing you can do is give your dog his first car ride experience to the vet!

- It often helps to have another dog in the car to keep his mind occupied. Dogs should be kept either on the back seat or in a contained area with a dog guard.

- A well trained dog (and it is never too late to start training) will not jump around in the car. It is basic safety sense to harness your dog if there is any risk – this also allows you to have a window open without the fear he'll jump out of the car.

- Don't let your dog stick his head out of the window as small flying objects can cause a nasty accident and a lot of wind can damage his eyes. If you have a convertible, make sure your dog is very secure and that he has been trained well enough to lie down.

- If you must leave your dog in a car, make sure it is for a brief period of time and that a window is open sufficiently enough for him to get air. Never take your dog in the car in very hot temperatures as dogs dehydrate rapidly. Keep a spare bottle of water in the car to give your dog after a long walk – the season of the year is irrelevant.

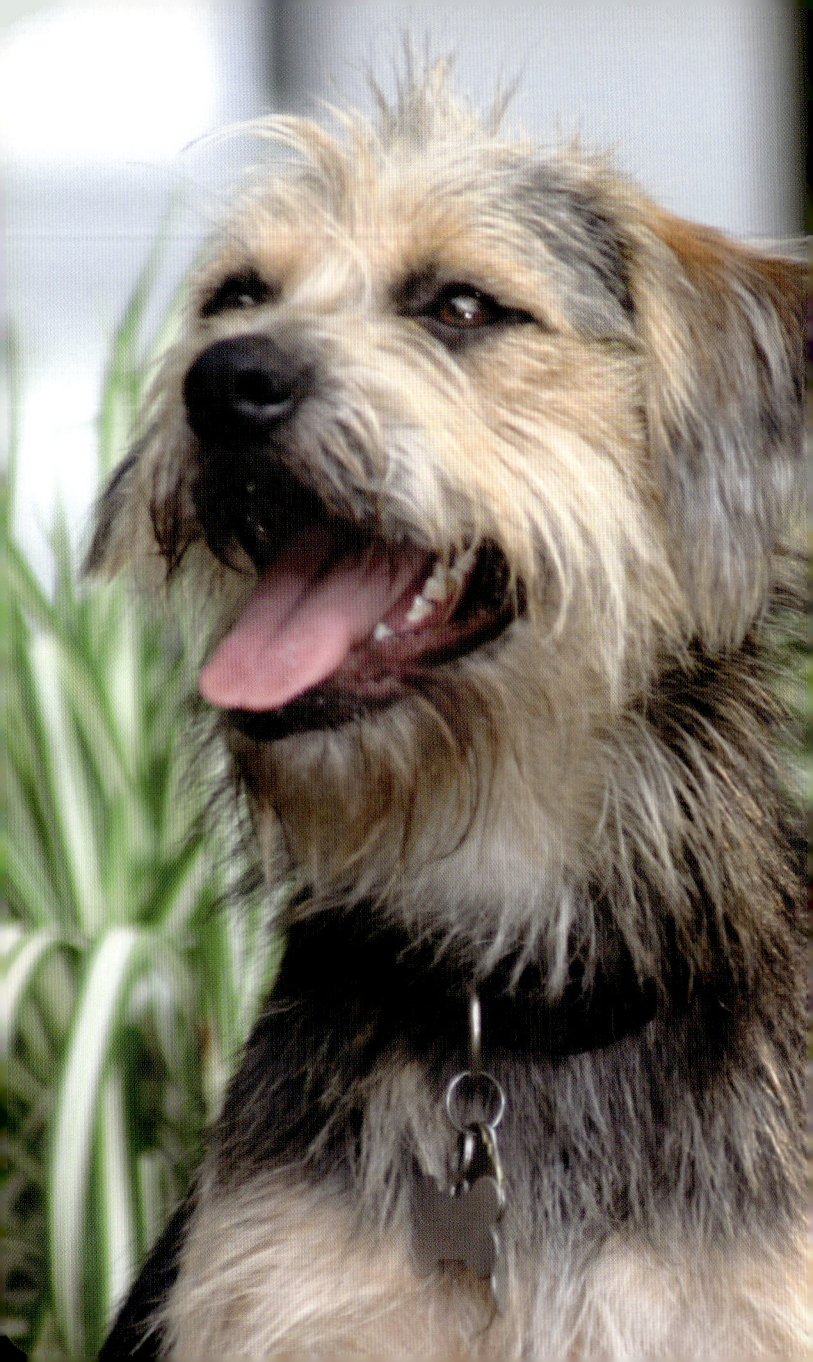

60 Real-life Dog Rescue Stories

It is clear from the entries in this book that there is nothing more gratifying than rescuing a dog and turning its life around. Most of the dogs in this book were saved from a living hell – some did not survive and that is the sad part about rescue. We cannot save the world of abandoned animals but if we make a difference to just one dog's life, it is one less dog on the street.

A dog will recognise a genuine dog lover. They are incredibly perceptive animals but having said that, it is their nature to try to please. If that love is abused, dogs stress, they get anxious. Like humans they grieve for lost pals and owners. I cannot stress the importance of realising that adopting a dog is like adopting a child. The whole family needs to support the idea of having a dog in the house and be willing to take on the commitment.

Iris

... The First Three Years

Iris was just one of the millions of hapless strays that live in the harsh, often cruel streets of Taiwan. When Iris was six months old, she was placed in an overcrowded shelter where she was neglected and mostly confined to a small crate in which her paw got caught and became twisted, resulting in a permanent limp. Because Iris hardly had any human contact, she became an intensely shy dog, unfamiliar with people and anything beyond the limited confines of the sanctuary.

... The Streets of San Francisco

The Animal Rescue Team in Taiwan learned of Iris' story and funded her flight to the US where a family would be waiting to adopt her. Just as Iris' plane landed, the family experienced a medical emergency and was no longer in a position to adopt her. Stranded at the airport, Iris ended up going home with Judy Nguyen, a rescue volunteer with Walkin' the Bark Rescue.

> "Iris has taught me that every dog, no matter how shy and scared, has the ability and desire to love and to trust. All they need is to be shown patience and gentleness, and for someone to simply give them a chance."

"Iris hid in the corner of the room, refusing to look at me and if other dogs approached, she'd back away shaking with fear. She was completely overwhelmed."

Iris stayed with Judy for 5 days until she was transferred to a more permanent foster home. However, three days later something scared Iris and she bolted from the home. Despite intense search efforts, Iris remained missing for 41 days before she was miraculously found by San Francisco Animal Care & Control.

… Learning to Trust

When Iris was finally found, starved, dehydrated and with half of her body weight gone, she returned to Judy's house. Although Iris had spent only five days there prior to her 41 day disappearance, she immediately recognized the home.

"Whatever timidity and fear Iris had towards me when she stayed here the first time around, and it was quite severe, vanished when she came back. All barriers between us crumbled and Iris came to trust me completely."

Home at last
Iris was finally adopted and now lives with Rob & Jen in Northern CA, along with their 2 cats and a massive puppy named Otis, who she delights in bossing around.

Annie

Orphan Annie

On October 13th, 2005 Limerick Animal Welfare managed to catch an Irish Lurcher they'd been after for two weeks. Wild and terrified, she'd been running around with a broken leg embedded with wood and barbed wire. Frightened of humans, she covered many miles to avoid being caught but her hunger and pain eventually got the better of her and she was cornered in a garden. Once secured, she collapsed and the volunteers carried her to an emergency vet. They named her Annie.

"Her leg was swollen to at least three times the normal size and the smell of rotten tissue and flesh was nauseating. The pain Annie must have been in – the weather was so cold."

Annie was just a year old and had no body fat whatsoever. Whoever had tried to splint her leg used timber and twine which had penetrated her flesh. The vet told Limerick that she would have to have the leg amputated.

The surgery started her on IV fluids, pain killers, antibiotics and sedatives. Annie was then re-assessed by two other vets and the decision was made to try and save the leg. They removed all the dead tissue and then dressed the leg. Her dressings were changed daily to encourage new tissue to form. "Gradually the wound started to granulate."

As the wound healed, new tissue grew to cover the exposed bone and Annie's circulation improved. When Annie was a little better, she was discharged to the home of Chris, a Limerick Animal Welfare foster mum where she continued to recuperate in front of the fire with a cat for company. Annie improved both physically and mentally, losing her fear and becoming quite outgoing. However, she needed to exercise her leg to encourage muscle growth and start physio and hydrotherapy. She needed a forever home with an owner who was willing to continue treatment.

New York State of Mind

Annie found her forever home with in Albany, NY with a loving couple who are well equipped to deal with Annie's special needs. Her mom is home all day and dad works in sports medicine at a local college. They have two young children and Annie also has three canine brothers and one sister. The males are a three-legged Lab called Dexter, Doc a retired greyhound and Zeb a nutty black Lab. Annie's sister is a Galgo (Spanish Greyhound) called Feliz.

Three Chocolate Girls

Jenny, Esther and Daisy are three very lucky chocolate coloured Labradors rescued from a puppy farm in London by The Labrador Lifeline Trust. All three had been used as breeding machines and when they were found were pitifully thin and unused to being handled. TLLT believe that Jenny and Esther were about three and Daisy was about six years old.

… Tip Off

TLLT received a call from a contact who tries to rescue dogs and breeding bitches from puppy farms and dealers. In Jenny, Esther and Daisy's situation, two members of staff were told to meet the contact in a back alley in North London near the house where all the dogs were kept. A van arrived and three dogs were unloaded and handed over to the TLLT representatives.

… What a State to Be In

All three were dreadfully nervous and were obviously no use for further breeding. Daisy was in the worst condition. She had a chronic skin condition bought on by stress. All her teeth were rotten and she had a cyst which was thankfully benign. Jenny and Esther were severely undernourished. All three were mute on their way back to the TLLT kennels.

… New Beginnings

None of the dogs had been vaccinated and had never been treated for any of their ailments. The Labrador Lifeline Trust immediately got the dogs vaccinated and Cheryl Sears, their vet began homeopathic treatment on Daisy's skin condition. Within one month, Daisy's coat was back to normal without steroids. All three dogs were kept at the kennels for four weeks not only to get them back into shape, but to de-stress and get used to regular human contact.

… Successful Adoptions

All three labs have been successfully re-homed. Esther went to a lovely home in Devon with a former TLLT helper and has a brother called Bob. Daisy now lives with another dog called Ellie and cats who think that she is just fabulous. Her new mom Lynne says that her confidence has come on in leaps and bounds. Jenny was adopted by Lyn Rhode and has a brother – a four year old lab called Toby.

> **Do's & Don'ts**
> DON'T be afraid to try homeopathic medicine but always check with your vet. More information on alternative treatment can be found at http://www.bahvs.com

"Her idea was to walk from side to side in front of me, stopping occasionally to look up. I suspect she might have done the same with her pups."

Lyn says that she has gradually put on weight, loves pigs ears – in fact is becoming a greedy Labrador! In her first week at Lyn's, Jenny had to have three short walks a day to build up her muscles, she has now gained confidence to explore, relax in her sleep and "she has a cute little snore." Thanks Anne at TLLT for this uplifting story and thank you adoptive parents for taking on older dogs.

Aesop

... September 17th, 2006

The state of the little black mongrel of undeterminable breed was so horrific, that even Limerick Animal Welfare, used to witnessing cases of extreme cruelty, were stunned at this display of human negligence. Limerick thought that Aesop was about two and possibly a poodle. It was impossible to tell as he had Sarcoptes mange so badly, that he had very few tufts of hair left on his tough as leather skin. His eyes were so badly infected that he was unable to open them.

> *"It took many long, lonely and painful months for Aesop to get into this state."*

Aesop scratched his hat rack thin body constantly. He was like a canine ghost and Limerick seriously doubted that they could keep him alive. The prognosis was so bad that even if they began treatment, the estimate for the vet's bills was prohibitive and Limerick's accountant told them that they simply did not have the funds. Limerick Animal Welfare, like so many rescue centres, are used to surviving on a shoestring budget and they hastily organized an Aesop fundraiser. They are well known in the area for taking in the worst cases of maltreatment and public response was terrific. They also have a 'no holds barred" website – graphic yes, but the facts are, these types of cruelty cases need to gain public attention.

When what was left of Aesop's hair was cut off Limerick discovered an infestation of maggots under his skin. With the help of donations, a radical treatment program was initiated and Aesop stopped scratching quite so much. He also began to tolerate small meals but his eyes continue to cause terrible anxiety. It was ascertained that he had a cataract in one eye – both remained very gummy with disease.

… October 1st, 2006

Aesop's skin improved and he gained a little weight. His character started to emerge but he was still critical. His plight had been noticed by other refuges and people continued to send donations. By October 8th, Aesop had stopped scratching and was overall, a much happier dog. His eyes continued to be a problem and he was put under the care of a homeopathic vet. Progress was slow but Aesop began to enjoy life, especially when he could pose in his dog jacket and go for a short walk. "One of his greatest pleasures is being strong enough to lift his leg again!"

... November 28th, 2006

Aesop began to grow a new coat and was ready to be re-homed. Once he began to take on a proper form, it was discovered he was a Kerry Blue Terrier. He did not get on with other dogs but was great around people. His favorite sport is football and once he'd gained enough weight, he loved nothing more than bounding after the ball at high speed.

January 25th, 2007 – Happy Endings

Over six months had passed since Aesop first came to Limerick Animal Welfare. He was a totally different dog and thanks to the tenacity of the people at Limerick, he was finally found a forever home.

Baggins

... One Angry Dog

Springer Spaniel Baggins is an undeniably difficult dog. He ended up at Springer Spaniel Rescue after his first family found him overly possessive and aggressive. Although he was in good condition, his behaviour made him almost impossible to be around. In fact he had been re-homed twice before; at only 16 months old, he went to adoptive parents who not only put up with his aggression, but have helped him to become relatively socially acceptable.

... Too Possessive

Baggins' parents, Sylvia and Colin, had not meant to adopt another dog – in fact they were dead against it having lost three dogs over the last seven years to illness and age. They were left with Gordon, a rickety 12-year-old Gordon Setter and were quite happy to leave it at that. Trawling the Internet changed the family dynamics when up popped Baggins on SSR's website. After lengthy consultation with Glyn at SSR, they were left with a very clear picture of the challenge ahead if they went ahead and adopted Baggins. They decided to try but would return him if he attacked Gordon. Baggins was not their first spaniel but even so, they were daunted by his hyperactivity and possessiveness.

... It's my Rolo

On the way back to their home in Scotland, Baggins caught a whiff of chocolate from a bag of Rolos. He lunged across from the back of the estate car and when Colin tried to remove the bag from his mouth, he bit him. This display of temper was just a taste of things to come.

... The First Night

Once home, Colin, Sylvia and Gordon tried to make Baggins feel welcome.

> *"The first night he trashed Colin's specs, a pillow, several magazines, tea towels, Gordon's bed, and several throw rugs."*

Colin and Sylvia thought that he had probably been beaten for his antisocial behaviour and learned not to try to take anything away from him. The first month was almost intolerable as Baggins continued to steal and destroy.

... Battle Scars

Although Baggins got on fine with other dogs, he continued to bite and it was touch and go whether or not he would have to be returned to SSR. Colin and Sylvia hung in knowing that this was realistically his last chance. Eventually, he learned to play ball and not destroy the house when they went out. An increase in exercise and being firm but not physical gradually gave Baggins the confidence he needed. Around month two, he started to show signs of reciprocal affection and

> *"there was light at the end of the tunnel."*

… Month Three

Baggins is still a challenge. He does sometimes torment Gordon and Colin and Sylvia still get the odd nip, but he now cuddles and is always rewarded for good behaviour. Instead of reacting when he is naughty, they ignore him so there is no mutual confrontation. Sylvia and Colin are in this for the long haul and know that bad behaviour will not change overnight. Baggins is incredibly lucky to have found two people who are willing to put in the time and energy to turn his life around.

… DO Realize

Some dogs will adapt quicker than others and realistically, most re-homed dogs will have emotional baggage. Springer Spaniels in particular need lots of stimulation and exercise and they need to know who is the Alpha in the family – you not them!

Do's & Don'ts
Do exercise your dog regularly – a trip around the garden is not sufficient for any breed. Remember that some dogs need 2 hours exercise plus per day. Don't buy a breed of dog that you cannot exercise accordingly.

A book I would highly recommend for behavioral problems is:
The Dog Listener by Jan Fennell

Fran

... Bred to Fight

Fran was brought to St Francis Animal Welfare from Southern Ireland in 2004. A Staffordshire Bullterrier puppy of only seven months of age, she had already endured a sad start to her short life; she was bred solely for the cruel and illegal sport of dog fighting.

However, Fran had not a malicious bone in her little body, and just wanted to play, as any normal puppy would. Because of this, her nasty owners decided to starve her, beat her and keep her locked up in a darkened, damp, shed. They shoved her in a tiny cage to try and get Fran to turn vicious. The malnutrition, cramped accommodation and lack of exercise caused poor Fran's legs to start growing deformed; she squatted in her cage, day in day out. As Fran started to deteriorate rapidly, someone tipped off a local dog-lover, Tess, a friend of St Francis, who regularly brings dogs over from Southern Ireland, because of the lack of animal shelters there.

Photography by Wendy Clinton

... Permanent Damage

Tess managed to convince the owners to let her have Fran, and took her to her own home. Although weak and traumatised from her experience, Fran slowly started to settle into a normal puppy's life. However, after her first trip to the vet, it was confirmed that Fran had sustained damage to both hind legs, and possibly her pelvis.

Tess brought Fran to St Francis Animal Welfare where she began physiotherapy to build her muscles and strengthen her bones. She had several operations – pins were inserted to straighten both her hind legs and to enable her to sit and walk properly. St Francis Animal Welfare does not receive any government funding, and Fran's treatment amounted to thousands of pounds. However, it is the shelter's policy never to put a healthy animal to sleep, so they never gave up on Fran. They launched a local appeal to find Fran a loving owner sure that her lively, cheeky personality would win someone over.

... The Altruistic Wakelins

When Fran was two years old, John Wakelin, a long-time supporter of St Francis Animal Welfare rang the shelter. John had adopted two dogs from St Francis in the past, Holly a German Shepherd, and Nutmeg, a Terrier cross.

He had been particularly impressed with St Francis because, despite the shelter having received requests for Holly and Nutmeg to be adopted individually, they had waited for the right owner to come along and accept both of them together.

They had been with each other from a very young age, and were best friends. Holly and Nutmeg had a wonderful life with John and his family, and now John wanted to give another dog the same chance. He asked the shelter manageress, Ann Hillman, whether they had a dog that was difficult to re-home. Of course, Fran came to mind, but would someone be willing to take on a dog with such physical and possibly emotional damage? John, his wife Hardip and their family decided to visit the shelter, to see Fran for themselves. The result?

> **Do's & Don'ts**
> DO report suspected organized dog fights.

"Love at first sight"

says John. They made an instant decision there and then to take Fran home.

... Solutions to Problems

John and his family quickly learned that Fran got terribly distressed if she was left on her own, especially the first time she was left in the dark. The solution was simple: leave a light on, so Fran could feel secure in her new home. The only sign now that Fran had a troubled past is the way she sits. She cannot bend her back legs like any normal dog can, and drapes them frog-like behind her (see photo)

... No Regrets

John says they have never regretted taking on Fran.

"I have never known a dog with such a fantastic and gorgeous personality. She is absolutely fantastic with children. You would never think that a dog that had been treated so cruelly, would be as loving and friendly as Fran."

Bambi

Bambi, a three-month-old Lurcher puppy, was rushed to Wood Green Animal Shelter in critical condition. She'd been found on the street homeless without identification. Dehydrated with chronic diarrhea, she was diagnosed with Parvo virus.

... Waiting Out Parvo

There is no cure for Parvo, a viral disease usually found in puppies. It attacks the intestinal lining and is often fatal. Bambi was given antibiotics and fluids to re-hydrate her. After three days, her appetite returned and there was no blood in her faeces. Six days later, she still had diarrhea so was given Protexin Powder too help digestion.

> **Do's & Don'ts**
> DO get your puppy vaccinated against Parvo.

... Day Fifteen

Although very thin, Bambi's health improved and she was given the all-clear by the vet. She was given her first vaccination (there is a series of Parvo vaccinations) and removed from the isolation unit.

... Adorable But

Because she had been found young, Bambi exhibited no disturbing signs and was found an adoptive home within three weeks. Two weeks later she was back at the shelter. Her adoptive family could not leave her alone – without her digging up the carpet and urinating everywhere they felt they simply could not cope. At the end of January, she was taken to her new home and, six months later, has settled in well and has stopped digging and peeing in the house.

Two Red Heads

... The Luck of the Irish

Brandy's first owners kept her shut in a bathroom – no way to treat any animal let alone a stunning Irish Red Setter. One day, a man came to work on the house and took Brandy back to his home – her owners were pleased to get rid of her.

Brandy's foster family made a few attempts to find her a loving home, but were so struck by her beauty and temperament they ended up keeping her. She became a quintessential part of the family and allowed to share their bed – naughty I know but… Brandy was happy and secure, an only dog and the focus of attention.

... Four Years Later Rocky Arrives

Brandy's owners decided to get her a playmate and went in search of an Irish Setter puppy at the Irish Setter show in Wayne, New

Jersey. They did not find a puppy but ended up adopting a huge skinny wreck from Irish Setter Rescue. Rocky had been found wandering around in some woods and was taken to a local pound. A family took him for only six months and then took him back. He was only two years old and full of whipworms; his fur had to be shaved as he was covered in burrs. Irish Setter Rescue of New Jersey took him from the pound and made the connection with Brandy's parents at the Irish Setter Show.

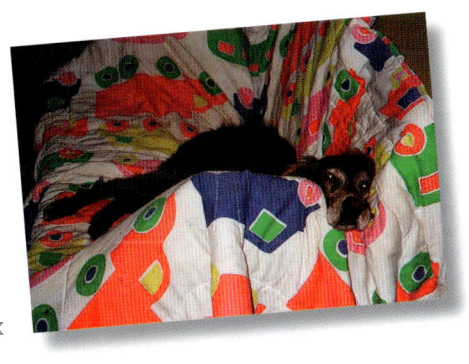

… Rocky's Recovery

> **Do's & Don'ts**
> DO get your dog wormed there are lots of products you can buy in your local pet store. They need to be regularly wormed about every 6 months.

Rocky was initially very sick and kept throwing up. His new parents cured him of his worms and got his coat sorted out. He soon gained 15 lbs and began to look like a proper Irish Setter – a much bigger version of Brandy. He had had no training and used to steal from the counter and jump all over the place. Brandy's stalwart nature had a calming effect on him and eventually he stopped rummaging around in garbage cans and learned to enjoy being a normal dog. He did chew up the training book his owners bought and puts their socks and shoes by the front door imagining that this would stop them going out.

… Little 'n' Large

The two Setters' have very different characteristics – Brandy is a bit on the porky side and at ten, is fed diet food and is far more sedate. Rocky has to be fed large portions of Canine ID to build up his strength and maintain his weight. Rocky hates the grooming clippers but is good at catching butterflies. Brandy is appalled at the camera's flash and distains squeaky toys while Brandy is passionate about his patriotic green ball. Although Brandy was jealous of Rocky at first interrupting her set routine, they now get on just great.

> *"He is so big that she can walk right underneath him."*

Irish Setter Rescue New Jersey provide endless support and the Setters' mom has replaced the training manual with videos because the hard plastic coating is not as tasty as paper.

Happy Times
Dogs are great therapy to the elderly; the dogs also enjoy the attention with lots of fussing. Some nursing homes actively encourage dogs coming in to visit patients.

Burlap

Burlap is a 5 year old Cairn Terrier who was picked up with another stray – a dachshund- by Sacramento County Animal Control over the Christmas period. Yet another unwanted holiday dog. The dachshund was adopted so Burlap was left all alone and sentenced to be euthanized. The director of Animal Savers' stepped in at the last minute to save Burlap from her lethal injection. She cried when she saw Burlap cowering against a concrete wall behind bars trying her best to make herself invisible. Poor Burlap was completely traumatized and was desperate to be with another dog for moral support and security.

... Foster Care

In the Animal Savers' facility, Burlap sought moral support with the other dogs and cats, but had a real problem with humans. She was so distressed that the director of Animal Savers took her home to her ranch in an effort to get Burlap used to human contact, slowly building up her confidence in a quiet environment.

Burlap is now housetrained, obedient and loves laps. She adores being with both cats and other dogs and has found the courage to come out of her shell when handled gently by humans. This fragile little dog was finally adopted by a teacher in San Mateo who fell in love with her sweet face and willingness to please.

Marmaduke

"It doesn't matter how long you have been involved in rescue, it never prepares you for the cases like this poor old girl, abandoned in a time of her life when she needed human friends the most."

Marmaduke, a large chestnut german short hair pointer was found wandering the eastern suburbs of Melbourne by a ranger and taken to the local pound. She had been seen on the same street for a week but no one had bothered to help her.

The pound has an eight day reclaiming period, after which animals are distributed to other shelters for adoption or, if the pound feels that the case is hopeless, the animals are euthanized. In Marmaduke's case, she was reckoned to be over fourteen and in terrible shape. She was riddled with arthritis and covered in tumors. Her nails were so long she stumbled and she had no teeth.

... Day 2

In 2004, Von Chalmers founded Victorian Canine Rescue, a facility that helps public pounds and shelters re-house dogs. Von was walking down the aisle of homeless dogs, looking for candidates to re-home when Marmaduke caught her eye. "At this stage, she had all but given up the will to live, had stopped eating, and only struggled off her bed to relieve herself. How could anyone let her get this way?" It was agony for Von to walk away knowing that Marmaduke had 6 days to live.

There was not much interaction
between the two although
Marmaduke did start eating again
and would get off her bed when
Von reached the kennel door.

… Day 8

Like a prisoner on death row,
Marmaduke's last day had arrived. Von was met
at the pound by a member of staff. She said, "You're not going to
believe this but the old girl has been waiting for you all morning
and eaten a huge anticipatory breakfast." And there she was,
with her emaciated body and toothless grin. Von took her into the
garden for a final walk. In floods of tears, Von phoned her partner
Andrew, whom, having seen the state Von had been in over the
previous week, told Von "to bring the old chook home."

… Eight Months of Happiness

Von had Marmaduke assessed by a vet who said she looked terrible
but was not in any pain. Over the next eight months, Marmaduke
gained weight and relished the security of her last home. She died in
November 2005.

*"We could only wonder what
she would have been like in her
younger years and how on earth
after all those years of love and
loyalty could her owner turn his
back on her. We were blessed to
have this dog enter our lives; her
gift to us was one that no amount
of money could ever buy."*

Bella

... A Black Day for Bella

On a 35 degree (95 F) summer's day, Bella was driven into the countryside, thrown out of a car and left to die. By sheer luck, the lane in which she landed backed onto the property of Rudi and Mariette Meinel.

"I heard the car's engine coming down the lane, stop, reverse, and then take off at high speed. I think someone may have tried to run over her but by the time I'd run up the hill she had dragged herself to the side of the road."

... Chasse Dogs

Bella is a hunting dog, bred exclusively for the French Chasse Season (September – February). When she was found, it was obvious from the size of her cracked, extended nipples that she had been used as a puppy machine as well as a working dog. Like so many of France's chasse dogs, it was evident that during the summer, she had been give just enough food to be kept alive in order that she would be desperate and aggressive once chasse season opened.

"She was a bag of bones, her cream and liver spotted coat filthy and her claws were so long from being cooped up in a pen that she could not walk properly. I guess she was about 2 years old and had obviously had several litters of puppies."

... Bella's Adoptive Parents

Mme & M. Meinel own a large piece of land where they house abandoned dogs. They have built dog runs, kennels and fenced off large parcels so that these dogs get the life they deserve. The Meinels, immigrants from Germany, have dedicated their lives to rescuing dogs and although they live in a house in a nearby village they frequently sleep in their caravan situated on their land, so they can be close to their dogs.

At the time I interviewed them they had 19 abandoned dogs. Mrs. Meinel told me that Bella had been one of her most disturbing cases.

> *"The man that dumped her could not have known about our dog home as we'd only just relocated here. I couldn't believe it but now, 10 years on, I have seen sights that make me ashamed to be human."*

Bella is still painfully shy and won't look you in the eyes. She loves the company of the other dogs but sticks close to the Meinels' heels. She is also terrified of loud noises. We have to keep her in during chasse season and thunderstorms because she must think that she's being sent back to her former life.

Happy Family
The Meinels do not look to re-home their dogs as most are too damaged mentally and physically to adjust. I watched Bella curl up on an old bed in the shade. She still looks impossibly sad and her body seems all out of line like a clothes rack that refuses to fold. I watched as Rudi gave her a kiss and told her that she was beautiful. Ciao Bella.

* Sadly, M. Meinel died during the writing of this book. Madame Meinel is trying to keep the kennels running single handed.

Buddy

Buddy, a Chesapeake Bay Retriever was put to work during his residence at the Canine Connections Rescue and Adoption facility in Snoqualmie, WA. Canine Connections operates a pet therapy program designed to save dogs from being put down, by using them in conjunction with the Echo Glen Children's Centre. Echo Glen is a juvenile correctional facility for adolescents aged twelve to twenty. Buddy was rescued by Canine Connections from his original owner who for three years had kept him chained up, sporadically pushing food at him. He got no affection nor exercise and was left to lie in his own filth.

... "Bad" Buddies

Buddy was paired up with a new handler, a hard-core ex-gang member, convicted of numerous crimes including cruelty to animals. Antisocial and skeptical, he was not thrilled to have an equally obnoxious, destructive and "unattractive" dog as his therapy partner.

"Buddy was not cool"

The counselors decided that the two were so alike, they just might learn from each other as both boy and dog needed social reconditioning.

... Makeover Time

Buddy's handler was taught about Chesapeake Bay Retrievers character traits, how to control Buddy's diet, get him used to being bathed, and how to groom him until he lost all his matted hair and his coat took on a shine. Most important of all, after positive reinforcement by Jo, the head counselor, his handler learned how to re-condition Buddy's negative traits. She told him "This dog would be a more loyal friend than any of his gang members would ever have been, that this dog would worship the ground he walked on and offer nothing but sincere devotion."

… Dual Growth

Buddy's handler began to see the loyalty and unconditional bond and friendship that Buddy could offer. As Buddy waited patiently by his kennel door, his tail pounding and his eyes fixed on his handler, the boy was amazed that anything could be so excited to see him, and they became inseparable. Jo was thrilled that this tough gang member showed his vulnerable side as he proudly boasted about his dog. "He now talks about his crimes and shows compassion and empathy."

… Showdog

Buddy also reaped enormous benefits from the program. He dropped 15 lbs, his runny eyes and smelly ears are now healthy and he lost about 3 bags of hair! But most of all, he too knows how to love and how to accept love.

… Graduate

Buddy has since been paroled to his new adoptive home and his handler felt good that Buddy had been given a second chance.

"When I was first assigned to Buddy, I judged him on his looks, not what was on the inside. I can see that I've done this all my life. If someone outside my gang was wearing other "colors" I was fighting the "colors" not the person. People are just like me inside. I learned a lot from my dog."

Fifi

... La Pauvre Petite

Alison Monk has a habit of rescuing dogs while on holiday. During her last vacation in Cotignac, Provence she saved the life of Fifi, a Yorkshire Terrier. She and a friend were driving through the country lanes when they saw a car sitting at the end of road that led to a wasteland. The driver threw something out of the window, revved up the engine and took off.

"When they saw us, they looked guilty, so we went to see what trash they'd dumped. To our horror, there was a small Yorkshire Terrier lying prone on the ground. She was not moving and was covered in ticks and fleas. Her body was emaciated and although she was breathing, was obviously in a pitiful state."

There were no other humans in sight, but there were some ducks and chickens pecking at the ground and across the other side of the wasteland, a small caravan. "We called out but got no response so we picked up the dog and took her back to our rental house."

The little dog was filthy dirty so they gave her a shower to get off some of the encrusted dirt and to wash off the fleas. They had to pick off the ticks separately. She ate some food and then just slept for hours. Fifi, as she was now called had absolutely no energy and Alison was not sure if she'd make it.

… My Hero, the Vet

Opposite the house was a Clinique Veterinaire so Alison walked across and told him her situation and asked his advice. The vet sent us to the local mairie (town hall) to see if anyone had reported her missing – if not, it was up to them. Needless to say, no one claimed her so Alison and her friend kept her at the house. As her energy level increased, they took her out with them to the restaurant in the evening and let her rest in the shade under the umbrella by the pool.

> *"She was really grateful to be near us"*

The next day they returned to the vet to see if they could pay for treatment and arrange quarantine to return to the U.K. This time, there was a different vet on duty and, after seeing the state of Fifi, said that he had plenty of land with a donkey, sheep and two other dogs and would be willing to take her.

> *"Fifi can keep me company during the day at the surgery and for house visits"*

Happy Endings
Alison and her friend returned to Cotignac last year to check up on Fifi. She was happily installed at the surgery and looked a different dog. Now a bundle of *joie de vivre*, she spends her days at the surgery being made a fuss of by the clients.

Freddie

... No Problems – We're on Vacation

Alison Monk was on holiday in Portugal with a friend when she first clapped eyes on Freddie. They were on their way to the beach looking forward to a relaxing day when she stopped at a shop to buy some water. Lying in the shop doorway was an emaciated cream colored dog. "People were treading over him as if he didn't exist."

Alison bent down to see if he was OK but he was in such bad shape, he could not even open his eyes. Her friend was not exactly a dog lover and told Alison to leave him – after all, thin abandoned dogs are a common sight in Portugal. Alison bought him some water and ham from the shop and reluctantly went off to the beach.

... Four Hours Later

When they passed by the shop having had enough of the sun, the dog had not moved and Alison was beside herself. When she stroked him, she noticed that he was riddled with fleas and covered in sores. She gave him some more water and ham which he managed to eat. "I was desperate and did not want to leave him." Very stressed, Alison returned to her apartment and the two of them got dressed up to go out for the evening. She tried to block the vision of the dog lying on the ground out of her mind and when they walked past the shop, the dog had gone. Alison hoped he'd found somewhere cool to rest for the night.

... Eyes Wide Shut

There they were, all togged up ready for a night out when they decided to take a shortcut through a gravel parking lot. There was the dog under a stationary truck. Alison went over to him and he managed to wag his tail. Much to her friend's annoyance, Alison decided she wasn't going out and would take the dog back to their apartment. Alison contacted a local vet who told her to bring the dog, now named Freddie, to their premises.

… Too Ill to Travel

Alison wanted to keep Freddie but after a thorough examination, the vet explained that he was simply too ill, that he had multiple health problems and it would cost a fortune to save him. Alison duly got out her credit card and paid for the treatment. The vet recommended that Alison contact a local Irish lady, a Mrs. Mucillhaggie, who rescued abandoned Portuguese animals. The next day, they met and instantly fell in love with Freddie and promised to look after him through his long quarantine, working with the vet to make him better until he could travel to England. Alison is indebted to Mrs. Mucillhaggie who sorted out the quarantine paperwork and required shots She also e-mailed Alison with progress updates. Freddie was finally able to travel and was met by an ecstatic Alison at Gatwick airport.

Lucy, Flora & Tara

Despite many articles published by the British Kennel Club and numerous adverse press reports, puppy farming continues to flourish across the UK and the USA. Lucy, Flora and Tara are three lucky West Highland Terriers rescued from various puppy farms in Wales by Ceredigion Animal Rescue & Education. They look like triplets in their photo, but are in fact, unrelated.

... Puppies to Order

These three Westies are typical examples of bitches used solely for breeding. These dogs often have nothing to look at in their concrete pens, or are shut up in dark, airless barns. When the dogs arrived at Ceredigion, they were in a pretty bad way – dirty and drained from endless pregnancies. They were immediately spayed, micro chipped and given shiny new collars.

"Of our three Terriers, it seemed that Lucy was the only dog comfortable wearing a collar. She was more docile than Flora or Tara, developing a confidence that soon rubbed off on the other two."

Lucy

Because she exhibited the most confidence, Lucy was sent to a foster family until a permanent home could be found for her. Although nervous around men, she had a blast swimming in her foster parents' pond.

Flora & Tara

Lucy's two compatriots were kept at Ceredigion until they had improved sufficiently to be ready for adoption. Ceredigion Animal Rescue & Education contacted Jaqui at Westie Rescue in Wiltshire to see if she could find homes for these three middle-aged ladies. Flora was seven and Lucy and Tara were around five. They also advertised the girls not only on their website, but with other reputable rescue homes in order to broaden the chances of finding a right home.

> **Do's & Don'ts**
> DO buy from registered, reputable dealers. Call the Kennel Club to verify all paperwork. If you are still in doubt, make a few calls to your local rescue centers and get their opinion. Not all registered breeders follow the rules.

… Jaqui Comes Up Trumps

The good news came quickly for all three dogs. Jaqui found three perfect homes and the applicants passed their checks without any hitches. The lives of all the dogs are followed up on a regular basis and they continue to thrive in the loving environments that they so rightly deserve.

Lucky

... Lucky To Be Alive

Lucky is a 3 year old cross Doberman Terrier. She is super fit and relatively well behaved. She lives in a tiny village in France surrounded by vineyards with a loving Mum and a rotund cat called Princess. She has not always been so lucky.

... December 2004

On the Thursday before Christmas, Lucky's owner Fiona was calling her family in England from her local phone booth. She noticed that a tiny shadow had snuck into the booth and was trembling at her feet. A black puppy with tan feet and matching eyebrows wriggled in delight at the respite from the bitter cold.

Back in Fiona's kitchen, the puppy proceeded to pee all over the floor and eat everything in sight. The next day, Fiona discovered from the *mairie* (town hall) that the puppy had been dumped out of a car three days prior. She then called the French SPA (animal rescue) but they failed to show up. That night, the temperature dropped to 23 degrees and if Fiona had not taken her in, the puppy would have frozen to death.

> *"She had no fat reserves, a very short coat and when she did a bowel movement, it was a mass of white seething worms. She was riddled with fleas."*

... Uphill Struggle

Lucky continued to mark her territory in the house, and even worse, she ate other animals' feces – any animal, even bird droppings. This was an indication that Lucky had survived this way, living outside processing faecal nourishment. "I've got a strong stomach but to watch her eating dog pooh really grossed me out." Lucky continued to eat – the car seats, the upholstery, and went nuts every time she wore a collar and lead. Unless she was on a lead, she ran away.

"She did not make eye contact with me for eight months. Despite the fact she loved children and other animals, it took ages for us to bond. I felt that I did all the giving with no response."

There were many days that Fiona felt like giving up. When Lucky was 10 months old, she went to obedience classes but the trainer believed in brandishing the stick with no reward for good behaviour. Fiona felt that Lucky's difficult but fragile spirit was being crushed, that she'd suffered enough in her first four months. She was terrified of noise so having someone yell at her when she would not sit was not the answer.

… Patience Pays Off

Although still defiant, Lucky has improved tremendously. She stays *aux pieds* (at heel) and is very affectionate to both Fiona and the cat, Princess, who accompanies Lucky for a short distance on their walks.

"She is Lucky to be alive, but I love her so much and that feeling is finally reciprocated. It's been a worthwhile haul"

Laddie

Sarah is a foster mum for Hope Rescue based in Neath, South West Wales. Like many rescue organizations, Hope has foster mums in various parts of the British Isles and Sarah lives in Suffolk. Hope works with a variety of other rescue shelters to help facilitate abandoned animals in finding foster mums and permanent homes.

Laddie, a beautiful Rough Collie puppy was sent to her for re-homing all the way from Ireland. Laddie, along with two other puppies, had been saved by a rescue facility who networks with Hope. It would appear that the puppies had been stolen by gypsies and were about to be sold on the street. The puppies had to be moved out of the area quickly as the gypsies had buyers already line up.

... A Toxic Bath

All the puppies had been thrown into a sheep dip containing Invermicin, a pesticide that is lethal to Collies. One can only assume that the gypsies, in their ignorance, thought that a toxic bath would kill lice and fleas. Hope arranged contacts from Ireland to England in order to save these poor babies. With the help of volunteers, all three puppies were transported by ferry to the UK where Hope foster parents were awaiting their arrival.

Once Laddie had been "detoxified" Sarah set about getting him fit and ready for a forever home. Unfortunately, the assigned family, who lived locally to Sarah, backed out of the adoption at the last minute when they heard that they had been approved to foster children. Sarah could not bear the idea of Laddie having to travel yet again to another strange home and decided to keep him. "He has remained with us as a very much loved and treasured member of our family." Laddie is now eighteen months old and as you can see from his photo, is loving life.

… Timing Was Crucial

This is another story where timing was crucial. If the volunteers in Ireland had not acted quickly, the puppies would have been sold on the street and Laddie would have most probably died of Invermicin poisoning.

Koshi

... Planning Ahead

In the summer of 1993, Doug and Sheryl Cochran made the decision that they would adopt a dog. They had to wait until they returned from an already planned trip through Nepal and Thailand, but during that trip, they found a name for their future family addition. The name Koshi came to them during a Himalayan trek; a Nepalese word for river. Now all they had to find a dog to match the name.

... Gold Rush

Early in 1994, Sheryl contacted Second Chance Animal Rescue in San Rafael, CA, and told them that she and Doug were looking for a dog with a golden temperament. They were matched up with a two-year -old Golden Retriever, then called Rosie, who had been found at the Lake County Pound. The Cochrans drove up from their home in Mountain View to meet with Deb from Second Chance in San Francisco. Second Chance Rescue offered to let the Cochrans keep Rosie overnight to double check that the match worked. Doug and Sheryl took one look at Rosie and knew that it would not be necessary and Rosie became Koshi.

... Take Your Dog to Work Days

With very few exceptions, Koshi went everywhere with the Cochrans, even business trips. "Sheryl cut short a Grand Canyon trip to come home to her. She said she needed to work but I never believed that." says Doug. Our longest stint apart was in 2000 when we traveled to China to adopt our daughter Enya. Koshi initially felt her nose had been put a little out of joint but "soon discovered the bounty under the high chair" and accepted her place in the hierarchy. The Cochrans educated Enya, their daughter, on what it meant if Koshi bared her fangs and they became fast, mutually respectful friends.

... Mouthful

Koshi had a passion for tennis balls; at one stage she was able to hold a record four in her mouth! She loved to camp with the Cochrans and was once on the receiving end when she chased some deer. Koshi learned to kayak and raft and chased the Cochrans back country skiing.

"It's hard to imagine a dog more loved, but I guess many families would claim that."

... Our Nemesis Called Age

Inevitably, as the years passed Koshi began to show signs of ageing. She had a benign tumor removed from her bladder but then she began to favor her left hind leg and had to go on pain meds. Getting up and down became an obvious struggle and life's pleasures began to slip away. In the summer of 2005, Koshi left the Cochrans to "chase that great tennis ball in the sky." Doug sent me this quote that epitomizes the love that the Cochrans felt for Koshi.

"He is your friend, your partner, your defender, your dog. You are his life, his love, his leader. He will be yours, faithful and true, to the last beat of his heart. You owe it to him to be worthy of such devotion."
– Unknown.

Harry

Ashlea forgot to "use protection" when she went with her younger sister who was looking to adopt a puppy. After an emotional visit to a local shelter, they heard that there were some additional animals to adopt at their local PetSmart. PetSmart (for non US readers) is a huge chain that sells everything for domestic pets and sometimes has "adopt a pet" days to help unwanted animals. They vet prospective candidates carefully, and once Ashlea's sister found the puppy she wanted, she began to fill out mountains of paperwork.

Do's & Don'ts
DO know that PetSmart is not a typical pet store and their adoption policy is rightfully stringent. They do a great job helping local humane societies and shelters find good homes.

... Just Looking

Ashlea decided to kill time by wandering around the store and stopped to pet the other dogs up for adoption.

"When I saw Harry I instantly fell in love with his dark eyes and scrappy hair so I kept walking!"

Her feet kept finding their way back to Harry's crate. Odd how that happens! Ashlea thought that Harry's mix of Schnauzer and Terrier was perfect, that his age and size was exactly what she would choose – if she was looking for a dog, but of course, she wasn't. He was very calm and gentle which, considering his start in life, was extraordinary.

… Harry's First Year

Harry had arrived in Hamilton County thin and completely bald and was sent over to the Hamilton County Humane Society. His front leg had been broken and because it had never been set, had caused it to heal crooked leaving him with a permanent limp. The Humane Society loved him and once his hair began to grow back, gave him his name. They told Ashlea that he was about a year old and had been in foster care. The foster family had introduced Harry to children, cats and made sure he socialized well with other dogs. They had to house break him as it appeared he had never before had a home.

An enchanted Ashlea made the fatal move of playing with Harry in the shop outside his crate and inevitably, he ended up going home with her.

"Single parenting wasn't easy at first but I am so glad I stuck it out. I can't imagine me without him now."

Rags to Riches

Harry is now the SpokesDog for the McKamey Animal Care and Adoption Center. He was featured in our 2007 calender and has made several TV appearances.

Heidi

Heidi's story is yet another account of the horrors of puppy farming. German Shepherd Rescue in Scotland had been tipped off about a man breeding German Shepherds in a high rise flat in Aberdeen. They were told that there were about 18 dogs cooped up with no outside space. The puppies were being fed on the wrong food and had worms. After pressure from the local council, the puppies were moved to a friend of the breeder's kennels. Unfortunately, no one checked that the conditions were any better.

… Out of the Frying Pan

German Shepherd Rescue made a surprise visit to the kennels in the guise of prospective buyers and were appalled. The kennels were a series of windowless wooden huts housing about 50 dogs and puppies. When GSR asked about a recent shipment of puppies from Aberdeen, the kennel manager was vague about his dog infantry and would not let them into the kennels to see the puppies.

Money Talks

After stating that they were interested in purchasing a puppy whatever the cost, they were shown two of the rescued German Shepherd puppies priced at $100 each! The dogs were on a hard floor run covered in feces and urine. Despite the fact that it was a sunny day, no other dogs were visible and in all likelihood, were kept in the dark 24 hours a day. The kennels did not appear to have any proper runs. We did not hand over any money for Heidi.

When it came to transferring the white puppy into our vehicle, the owner put a rope lead around the puppies neck and then dragged her choking across the yard through puddles and mud. She would not let us help.

> **Do's & Don'ts**
> Don't buy your dog from a puppy farm – if you want a pedigree, make sure that the breeder is registered and can show you valid paperwork. Visit the kennels – never meet someone half way for convenience sake.

"The kennel claimed the puppy had a name and yet the dog appeared neither to recognize the name or be familiar with the kennel owner. The puppy was terrified which was very distressing to watch."

Only one other puppy survived from the original litter in Aberdeen. The kennel manager informed GSR that the others had been in such bad condition that they had to be destroyed.

Henry

Henry is a black and white Jack Russell Terrier who was dramatically saved by firemen from his home when it caught fire. His owners escaped and left him in the building. The firemen took him to the local police station who then bought him to Battersea Dogs & Cats Home where he was nicknamed Sooty.

Henry had been badly injured in the fire and was rushed to the emergency vet. One of his front legs had been so badly broken that it had to be amputated. Henry recovered well from the operation and was sent to Battersea Dogs & Cats Home, Old Windsor to recuperate. Set in the royal countryside of Runnymede, Henry was taken for quiet walks to build up his strength and to find the confidence to walk on three legs. Without the bustle of hundreds of other dogs he managed to physically readjust and to put his terrible ordeal behind him.

… Henry the Wonderdog

In August 2006, Henry was adopted by Dave Nicholson and Margery Thorogood as a much wanted pet for their daughter, Gemma. When they first saw him lying down in his kennel they knew immediately that he was the one. "Oh, said the lady, you mean the three legged one." When the lady bought him downstairs, the Thorogoods were amazed at how well he coped – they had had no idea when they saw him in the kennel that he was missing a limb.

The family had grown up surrounded by dogs and cats and when their German Shepherd died, there was a hole in the household that Henry was able to fill. Battersea are justifiably very particular about who adopts their animals.

"A lady came round and inspected our house. We had to raise the fence at the bottom of the garden and get a dog gate so that Henry would not go upstairs and eat Vera (the cat's) food." Because Dave is retired, he could spend the necessary time working with Henry.

> *"What I like about Henry is that he is good with kids, does not snap or take out his affliction on them. He has a growl sometimes when you get him off the bed."*

... A Pub Regular

The Thorogoods live bang in the middle of Windsor and Henry particularly likes being petted by all the pretty girls that pass by on their way to the corner pub. In fact, Henry is often found in the pub.

Cushings Disease
Henry has been recently diagnosed with Cushings Disease, a disease caused primarily by pituitary tumors. The disease is more common in older dogs – the Thorogoods were told Henry was around six but the vet thinks he could be older. The disease mimics typical signs of ageing. Symptoms can also mimic other ailments – frequent urination, hair loss, high blood pressure and nervous system disorders. It is not an easy disease to diagnose and requires a specific blood test. Although there is no cure, Henry is doing well on his drug regime and the neighborhood has rallied around to help. Dave was given a "dogmobile" as Henry cannot walk very far. With his special "go cart" "He is able to go to his old haunt, the pub, and get lots of attention. He still scampers along often getting his remaining front leg tied up in his lead." You can view Henry's unique gait on Dave's video website at:
http://www.divshare.com/download/1145835-936

Hilda

After weeks of Internet searching, the photo of a little black and white Terrier mix struck a chord in Kitty Fleichman's heart. Hilda, a twelve – year – old sweetheart was posted for adoption on Second Chance Animal Rescue's website – Kitty's search was over.

Second Chance Rescue had rescued Hilda, along with three cats and a dead rabbit from an abandoned locked van in Oakland.

> *"She smelled like death when she was pulled out. She had barely any teeth left and after an examination, was found to have a heart murmur."*

... Going to California

Second Chance Rescue kept their fingers crossed that Hilda would survive and were worried in any event that she would be thought too old to find a forever home. When Kitty first contacted them, they continued to worry because Kitty lived in Boise, Idaho, 650 miles from the Bay Area and her foster home.

... Too Frightened To Go By Plane

A friend offered to drive Kitty and Hilda back from California – Hilda was way too frightened to go by plane. As it was, Kitty held Hilda in her arms for the whole trip home. When Hilda finally arrived at the Fleichmans', she inspected the house, looking thrilled to have found such loving parents.

> **Do's & Don'ts**
> DON'T limit your search for your perfect dog to the shelter "next door". There are unlimited animals without homes so make the effort to search further afield.

Kitty takes her to work and each morning, she dances on her four white paws in anticipation of another pain free day. "Her tail arches up over her back is if to say 'Look at me! Second Chance Rescue aren't sure who is more thrilled, Hilda or the Fleichmans, but that 650 miles was sure worth the gas.

Humphrey

As you can see from his pose, Humphrey is a big guy, even for a British Bulldog. He weights 75 lbs and is now nearly seven years old. Boxer Angels Rescue took him from a family that found him too much to handle. They in turn had rescued him from a high-kill shelter.

... Bull In a China Shop

Humphrey will be the first to admit that his manners could do with a polish. "He tends to get a bit drooly after a long drink, so we always keep a towel handy to wipe his face." He is extremely strong and challenges the weak. Humphrey needed to find adoptive parents without children who could cope with his larger than life personality and his stubbornness.

Humphrey's Winston Churchill gruff persona masks the puppy inside. He loves bones, a tug of war, and dog cookies.

> *"He has never really mastered the fetch game though – oh well"*

Humphrey sits when asked but sometimes doesn't care to get up again and refuses to budge. He also barks a lot to get attention, but if ignored eventually shuts up. He is at his best outside in a big yard as his size can create havoc in the house.

... Lots of Excercise

Like so many big breeds, British Bulldogs need strenuous exercise and a petite patch of garden is no good to them.

Happy Endings

Humphrey found his forever home in July 2007 – a family that met all his requirements. They are taking him to formal training classes and making sure that he knows who is boss. After being shunted around for the first 6½ years of his life, it looks like Humphrey has met his perfect match.

Do's & Don'ts

Do feed your dog a balanced diet with moderate fiber content. Depending on the breed and age, some dogs benefit from being fed several times a day. Always feed your dog in the same place in a calm atmosphere.

Kane

Judy and Robert Findlay work for DCH Animal Adoptions in Australia. They specialize in rescuing and re-homing Rough Collies – the Lassie collies we are all familiar with from the T.V.

... Stunted Growth

The Findlay's received a call from their local pound who said they'd had a three-year-old sable and white collie bought in. His fur was so disgustingly matted, he had to be shaved. When the Findlay's arrived to collect him, the pound said they thought he was about eight years old. However, Kane had been starved (he weighed under 14 kilos) and had never had enough food to develop any muscle. Without his fur, Kane was so thin and malformed, that there was no trace of visible muscular development. He was in fact eight years old.

"His coat had been matted for so long that his feet were deformed as he could not walk properly. His back was being dragged down from the twisted knots around his hind legs. His tail was broken and he had a lump on his chest which turned into a weeping abscess."

… An Operation

Kane required an operation to remove the lump it had been there so long plus he had to have laser treatment every six weeks to help with severe arthritis of the bone due to years of neglect. Kane spent three happy years with the Findlays but sadly passed away on 18th November, 2006 after contracting terminal cancer.

> "Rest in peace dear, sweet Kane, you will be missed so much and will never be forgotten."

Do's & Don'ts
DO remember to groom your dog on a regular basis. Some breeds require daily grooming so be prepared to put in the time.

Jimmy

Jimmy is a deaf and cataract ridden 14 year old poodle (a *canishe* in French). When he was about 6 months old, he came within an hour of being tossed in a river because he was not an aggressive enough guard dog.

... Jimmy's First 6 Months

When Mrs. Gonzalez first saw Jimmy, he was being dragged along the road by a short bit of string by his current owner, a gypsy who lived near by. Blood was trickling down his chest where the string had cut into his neck. He was emaciated and covered in faeces. Because Jimmy never barked or whined she had not noticed the puppy before although she later found out that he'd been chained up with no water in the gypsies' back yard. On a good day he been hurled a handful of leftovers.

... Lifesaver

Outraged, Mrs. Gonzalez asked the gypsy where she was taking her *petit chien*. The coldhearted gypsy replied "He's a useless guard dog so I'm going to throw him in the river."

> *"He was about six months old, dehydrated, obviously close to starvation and cringed when I bent down to pick him up. I think he'd been regularly punched in the face. I already had a dog so I asked my son José if he would take him."*

José took one look into Jimmy's chocolate button eyes, at his filthy matted coat, wrapped Jimmy in an old sweatshirt, and took him straight to the vet who did not think Jimmy would last the night. However, after a week of intense treatment, José was able to finally take him home.

... Starting Over

Jimmy slowly, very slowly has regained confidence, although even today, he cowers when you go to stoke him.

> *"His deafness had been caused by repeated physical abuse and he is still pathetically eager to please. I take him to work with me as he is terrified of being left alone."*

Do's & Don'ts

DO Take Action. Jimmy is one lucky dog. Many people who abuse animals hide their cruelty in back yards or keep them chained up in the house. When Mrs. Gonzalez challenged the neighbors whose house overlooked the yard, they admitted that they had seen Jimmy and several other puppies which had since disappeared but were scared to report the incidents for fear of reprisal.

DO – report incidences of cruelty – you can ask to remain anonymous.

Leroy

... September 2005 – Hurricane Katrina

I don't think that anyone will ever forget the nightmare of Hurricane Katrina. The aftermath of the September 2005 flooding left thousands of animals homeless. When Julie Goff heard that Operation Kindness, a no kill shelter in Texas was about to receive animals from New Orleans, she signed up to be a foster mom.

Within a week, Julie received a call from the Foster Co-Ordinator to say there was a Chihuahua/Terrier mix scheduled to be euthanized. He had been a stray in New Orleans and all the shelters within the vicinity were overwhelmed trying to reconnect animals with their families. This poor little boy was about to be overlooked because he was not very healthy and no one had claimed him.

Leroy, as Operation Kindness had named him, was about two and heartworm positive. He also needed to gain some weight. Julie's job as foster mom was to get him healthy and put him up for adoption.

... He Can't Go Back ...

Wrapped in a blanket, Julie introduced Leroy to her husband who swears "It was love at first sight." They settled him in the guest bedroom with soft blankets and his food. "We spent time petting and talking to him and then left him alone to get some much needed rest." They made the joint decision that Leroy would never see the inside of a shelter again.

"Leroy has become my husband's best friend and my darling little clown."

Mazzel

Mazzel has a great life. He lives in Holland with his parents Boris and Miriam and is one of those dogs that you sometimes see on T.V. talkshows, lounging on a large, plush couch wedged in between the guests and interviewer. Looking at him today, it is hard to believe his horrendous story.

Mazzel was found by Boris and Miriam when they were on holiday on the popular island of Skiathos in North East Greece. He had been dumped in a trash can by the airport.

… The Worst Case I've Ever Seen

Helen arrived on the scene and couldn't believe her eyes. The dog had multiple wounds all over his body and several large holes in his head. He was crying and obviously very weak. He was crawling with maggots and you could see his bones shining through the holes. The three of them got the dog into the car and rushed him to the shelter. Miriam and Boris told Helen that they'd take him home with them to Holland – if he survived.

… Just a Baby

Mazzel was given a steroid shot and then Helen and her helper Jan set to work cleaning off the maggots. It took 3 hours. He did not want to eat so he had to have fluid syringed into him as there was no drip. The next day he was able to drink by himself but over the next couple of weeks, all his fur and skin on his head, neck and shoulders came off. " When we had first seen him I had thought he was an old dog some bastard had tossed in the bin, but when he first licked my hand, I noticed his lovely white teeth and realized just how young he was. Eventually, he was allowed to accompany Miriam and Boris home to Holland.

Ici

... Romanian Refugee

Ici is an adorable two-year-old mongrel who was sent to Battersea Dogs & Cats Home in London all the way from Rumania. His past is hazy – he was certainly beaten and neglected prior to being sent to a rescue home in Rumania who then sent him, along with a group of other abandoned dogs, to Battersea in July of 2006. Ici was terribly nervous of people, especially men and hates making mistakes indicating he has been severely punished and possibly tortured in the past. To this day, he is particularly nervous of trucks, men and loud vehicles.

... Tuesday, August 22, 2006

Nikki Weir and Andy Woolhouse arrived at Battersea for their "prospective parent" interview – they knew that they wanted to adopt but had not selected a dog. By this time Ici had been at Battersea six weeks – the rest of the Rumanian dogs had all been adopted. He was introduced to Nikki and Andy by his specially assigned volunteer Dave, who had worked hard to strengthen Ici's fragile self esteem. "After lots of cuddles, good food, Ici's personality started to shine through." Because he was so nervous, Ici had been moved to an outside dog run away from visitors and other dogs. Nikki and Andy could see that Ici would require a lot of patience, but the next day, after a veterinary check up, Ici left with them for his new home in Essex.

... August 23, 2006

After leaving Battersea's Rehoming Block, Nikki and Andy managed to get a very nervous Ici into their car and settle him on a comfy blanket on the back seat. He was sick on the way back to their house.

"Ici gave us a big, sorrowful look after his little accident; having endured the London rush-hour, Ici was thrilled to see his new bed and a bunch of toys waiting for him in the house."

... Tag Time

Ici followed Nikki and Andy everywhere and when they went to bed, he followed. They eventually managed to get him to sleep in his own bed but had to put it on the landing outside their bedroom door. During the next three weeks, Ici acclimatized to his new home. Little by little, with plenty of parental positive reinforcement, he became less nervous. Nikki and Andy are now taking him to classes which have helped him interact with other dogs and given him basic command training.

... And Since Then

In March 2007, Ici gained an adopted sister, a Border Collie/Golden Retriever mix called Molly. Ici has also appeared as a success story in the Battersea Cats & Dogs Home *Paws* magazine. He continues to thrive under his parents loving care and sends a huge "thank you" to the Battersea staff for giving him a second chance.

Markus

"Free to good home" read the advertisement. Markus, a Rough Collie, was taken by a woman, who over the ten months that she had him, allowed him to be attacked by her dog and let his coat become matted and filthy.

When Judy Findlay from DCH Animal Adoptions based in Sydney, Australia rescued him, she was appalled at his neglect.

> *"He had not been brushed the entire time that this woman had had him. He had more flea dirt than coat and his ears had been eaten off at the tops by flies. He had massive sores that bled and he was very underweight."*

Markus was only five years old and, when Judy had him checked out by the vet, he was OK except for an infection in both eyes. Judy went to work cleaning Markus' sable and white coat and feeding him up. "He was an easy going boy and loved to chat about his day."

Robyn and John Fisher had already contacted Judy, who specializes in rescuing Rough Collies. However, they were very positive that they wanted a female. Undeterred, Judy told them about Markus saying he was one of the most lovely collies she'd ever come across and that he'd endured terrible hardship.

Do's & Don'ts
DON'T give your pet away to just anybody because it's convenient. VET the home before taking any further steps. I appreciate that situations change and sometimes you have to give up your pet but put yourself in the animal's shoes.

Contact your local rescue home with a no kill policy and see if they can help.

Robyn Fisher called Judy back and having heard more about Markus, she and her husband were on their way to see him. Arriving two and a half hours later, they came face to face with Markus. Robyn cried because he looked so like their late collie, Zoe. John took Markus' face in his hands, looked into his eyes and promised "You'll never want for anything."

The Fishers renamed Markus "Beau" and were over the moon. Beau is ecstatically happy and gracefully received all the neighbors and their pets who came over to welcome him.

... A Word from the Fishers

"Not a day passes that we don't tell him how lucky we are to have him with us. I know that the awful memories are begining to fade ... there is a definite strut in his step when he patrols the property each morning."

Matsi

... Call of the Wild

Thomas "TJ" Benin is crazy about wolves so when Matsi, a rescued Siberian Husky entered his life, it was a dream come true.

TJ first saw Matsi (Matsi means sweet and brave in Blackfoot Indian) in the ER at the Noble Veterinary Clinic in Hayward where he works as an assistant. Her history is hazy to say the least. She was forcefully taken from owners who had starved her – TJ is not sure by whom exactly but she arrived at the clinic in a critical state. Matsi's foot pads were practically non existent so she may have once been a working dog up in Alaska and sold on to some unscrupulous owners.

> *"Her body shape was anything but pretty; filthy dirty and skinny to a point where her stomach and hip curves were actually dents. She was in horrible condition with brown smudge marks all over her white fur."*

... Step 1 – Fostering

After treatment, she was moved to the Oakland Animal Shelter. Because her body had been so abused, they initially believed that she was about seven years old. After she began to get a little better, a second diagnosis put her at age two or three. When TJ enquired about fostering, the shelter said that they did not foster dogs aged two years or older. TJ kept making calls until finally, Gail de Rita, head of fostering at Northern Californian Sled Rescue (Norsled) offered to help him. Because of her efforts and TJ's persistency, he was able to legally obtain Matsi from the Oakland Shelter.

"Fostering through Norsled has been great. They've been supportive in everything including getting food and financial support"

Thanks to being a loving and knowledgeable foster parent, through Norsled TJ was able to change his status from foster to adoptive parent.

… One of the Pack

Matsi is adored by TJ's roommates and melts hearts whenever TJ takes her on her lengthy walks. She needs a lot of exercise, loves to play chase, hide things in the garden, and socialize with other dogs. She sleeps in TJ's room – beside him or in her special crate bed.

"She's not an expert-tricks dog but she's the type that wants to be by your side until the very end."

Do's & Don'ts
DO ask about fostering. It does not necessary mean that the dog will at some point be taken away.

Max

... Reporting Cruelty

In January 2005, Paul Williams, a Chief Inspector with the RSPCA Solent received a call about a dog being abused in Portsmouth. Thank you to the person that called because Paul, familiar with animal suffering, was horrified and could not even tell that Max was a Golden Retriever, he was in such atrocious condition.

He went into the house and was shown the dog who had hardly any fur. Instead of a normal coat, the dog was a mass of sores and scabs and was so lethargic that he showed no interest when Paul bent down to examine him. "Paul immediately cautioned the owners and when he carried out an interview, it transpired that Max was only two years old instead of the fifteen he looked."

... Photographic Evidence

Max was removed from his owners and taken straight to the vet. The vet said that it was the worse case of cruelty he had seen in thirty years of practice and was astonished that Max was only two years old. He took some skin samples and gave Max pain relief. "Max had been woefully neglected and would take many months to put right." And this was just the physical side. What sort of mental damage had that couple inflicted? Max was taken to The Stubbington Ark Animal Shelter and boarded as a "Case Pending" for the Inspectorate. Photographs were taken as evidence against Max's previous owners.

... Punishment – But Not Enough

The staff at Stubbington were equally shocked by Max's appearance and he required intensive care by way of baths and medication. After such a long period of abuse, his recovery was slow.

> *"Max's case was heard at Portsmouth Magistrates Court in July and the owners pleaded guilty to causing Max unnecessary suffering by omitting to provide him with necessary care and attention."*

The court was appalled by the photos and considered a prison sentence. Unfortunately, Mr. Tate and Miss Shaw were only sentenced to 180 hours community service – not enough. They were however, banned from keeping any animals for life.

Max has been adopted by Janet Gilbert who works hard reassuring him life is worth living. She wrote to me about having Max in her life and how each little improvement in Max's mental and physical health bring her priceless moments. "It has taken a lot of patience and understanding to get Max settled … he is praised every day and has a structured existence." Max has been told by the children at the school opposite his house that he has "street cred" as during the winter, due to not having an abundance of hair, he wears a variety of coloured scarves.

Meg

... Cold Hearted Relatives

Meg is a beautiful eleven year old black Labrador who was devoted to her elderly owner whom she had been with from puppyhood. Unfortunately, the owner became ill, suffering from dementia, and needed to go into residential care. Her relatives did not want to take care of her, and despite her pleas, Meg's Mum was put in the home.

Unable to take Meg, her beloved dog with her, the owner pleaded with her family to care for Meg which they promised to do. However, they had no intentions of doing this, and had planned to have Meg put to sleep on the same day that their mother went into care. None of the local rescues were interested in taking an elderly dog, stating that

> *"They are too difficult to re-home"*

... We'll Take Her

When Farplace Animal Rescue heard about Meg's plight, they were only too pleased to take her in. Farplace does not have kennels as such. Like many rescue organizations, they place animals in foster care until a suitable forever home can be found. Meg's owner's relatives dropped her off at a Farplace foster home and told her poor owner that

> *"Meg is having a holiday at a friend's house"*

They left Meg, along with a blanket, food for a week and a

Do's & Don'ts

Do feed your dog a balanced diet with moderate fiber content. Depending on the breed and age, some dogs benefit from being fed several times a day. Always feed your dog in the same place in a calm atmosphere.

tiny donation with her foster family. They offered to pay for future vets bills "as long as they were not expensive" and told Farplace that their mother

> *"Had vast amounts of money stashed away and to ask her for some"*

... In Foster Care

Although Meg has a laid-back personality, she was naturally a little shell-shocked to find herself in a new home after so many years with one owner. Her foster mum already had two permanent dogs – a Border Collie and a Dalmation. They all got along splendidly and her foster mum is seriously considering making Meg a permanent resident. Meg has regained her figure – her owner used to forget how many times a day she'd fed her. She is very loved and Farplace hope that she will spend the rest of her days with her new family.

Murray

Martyn and Angela Baish became volunteer dog walkers for Maxi-Care, a rescue home in Grendon, Northants in 2004. The Baishs had never intended to adopt a dog as they already had three Boxers of their own but in early 2007, Maxi-Care was badly flooded so the dogs had to be found temporary accommodation until the problem was solved.

... Just for 3 Nights

They were asked if they could take Murray, a huge Boxer/Great Dane cross with whom Martyn was already familiar. Because of his strength, it was Martyn who'd been assigned as Murray's dog walker. He'd been at Maxi-Care three years and was a frustrated soul who did not get on with other dogs. They were understandably apprehensive and took him on an emergency basis for three nights until Maxi-Care's kennels could dry out. Unfortunately, England received another monsoon style downpour and the kennels flooded yet again. This time, Murray stayed at the Baishs for seven nights.

... Maintaining a Strong Bond

When Murray was returned to Maxi-Care, Martyn used to pick Murray up on Wednesdays and return him on Saturdays, thus maintaining a strong bond. He'd take Murray fishing with him and naturally, Murray hated leaving and it became more and more of an emotional wrench.

... April 2007

In April of this year, the Baishs decided to take Murray in on a permanent basis until he could be re-homed with a forever family. Although Murray is a warm and generally kind dog, he still has a problem with the Baishs three Boxers. In order to make things work, they insulated their garage and installed heating to make a palatial kennel. As Angela Baish states,

> *"He is now my husband's constant companion. Through patience and hard work, Murray has changed into a loving dog ... he certainly has come a long way."*

Do's & Don'ts

DO train your dog! Proper training is critical to both the dog's the owner's and the general public's welfare. All dogs are trainable and the younger you start, the better.

Leo and Oscar

… In Praise of Older Men

In October 2006, two Yorkshire Terriers, Oscar and Leo, were bought by police to the Wood Green Animal Shelter at Godmanchester (their headquarters). The dogs' owner had died and a neighbour had notified the local police who contacted the shelter to arrange collection. Wood Green had a hard task. Leo was already fourteen and Oscar ten. They had always lived together and could not be separated.

Leo had a testicular tumor and had to be castrated. Oscar suffered from increased liver enzymes and both dogs' coats were so badly knotted that much to their mutual horror they had to be shaved. Because he was so little, Oscar had to suffer the indignity of wearing a pullover to keep him warm and both dogs had to have dental work.

… Very Shy

Leo was very shy of strangers, yet loved to be cuddled, yet Oscar was quite the reverse. He hated to be picked up and made it quite clear to the shelter staff that he preferred his legs to touch the ground.

… Huge Challenge

Neither dog had been house trained nor had any interaction with other dogs or children. Wood Greens quest for new parents was looking more and more ominous. After three months, Wood Green found Leo and Oscar's new family – a loving couple who were prepared to adopt dogs with issues and in their twilight years.

... 6 Months Later

At the ripe old age of fourteen, Leo is still playing with toys and is a real lap dog. Oscar prefers to lie at his owners' feet and snore. Both make regular visits to Wood Green Shelter to support the other animals still waiting for their forever homes.

> **Do's & Don'ts**
> Do buy your dog its own toys and something to chew on – it is not OK to chew clothing or furniture

Clyde

... His First Year

For the first year of his life, Clyde was chained to his kennel, rarely fed and when that rare occasion arose, was fed leftovers. He was found by the Camano Island Shelter who then contacted BullsEye Dog Rescue, asking them to find him a permanent home.

"When Clyde first came to us, his skin was purple from bruising and his black fur really sparse. His ears were swollen with layer after layer of infection. We called him the Purple People Eater although he was the gentlest puppy on four legs."

Photography by Becky Meigs

> **Do's & Don'ts**
> DO know that BullsEye partner's with pit bull friendly animal shelters in the Puget Sound region to help promote breed knowledge, develop sound adoption practices, and find forever homes for homeless bully breeds. Pit bulls have an unjustified poor reputation. Many have been abused and neglected to encourage aggression – the owners are at fault not the dogs. There are now thousands of abandoned pit bull dogs and puppies that need help. Please see the Acknowledgement Page for just a few of the pit bull rescue organizations that need your support.

Clyde had not had a chance to have a puppyhood so although he was already one year old, he needed to be trained from scratch. Jennifer and Gretchen worked really hard with him. His sharp intelligence soon adapted to discipline and coupled with the TLC and good food dished out by BullsEye, Clyde was ready for adoption.

… Livingston I Presume

Clyde was quite the attention seeker. He loved children and at street fairs and on market day, he drew a large crowd who would stand in line to give him a tummy rub.

> *"Even though he was short (for a pit bull) and had a bobble head, people loved him. He was also unshaken by even the meanest dog barking in his face."*

Along came the Livingston family, Jeff, Melissa, Austin, Jacob and their three cats. They adore Clyde and he has slotted into their family with the greatest of ease. BullsEye Dog Rescue was thrilled that Clyde had found the perfect family.

Petey

... November 7, 2005

"Petey was one of the saddest cases I've ever seen," says Cindy, Petey's foster mum who works for Texas Old English Sheepdog Rescue. Her connection with Petey began on November 7, 2005 when she received a call from Melvin at the Houston SPCA about an Old English Sheepdog who had been turned in by its owner. He thought that the dog was old and probably had terrible skin problems.

When Cindy arrived at the SPCA she was shocked. Petey was covered in Sarcoptic mange, with most of his hair missing or dead. He had the longest tail and was rail thin…. "the most emaciated dog I have ever seen."

Cindy asked the SPCA to hang on to Petey until she could locate a foster home. She knew that this would be difficult – finding a completely isolated home as Sarcoptic mange is a very contagious parasite for both humans and other dogs. A fellow rescuer put Cindy in touch with Malise of Great Pyrenees Rescue who quickly offered to house Petey until he was no longer contagious.

... Just a Whippersnapper

Petey turned out to be only about one year old. Thanks to his iron constitution and will to recover he made some progress. Building him up took time. Malise fed him three small meals a day of boiled rice and chicken plus nutritional supplements to build up his immune system. He had a voracious appetite and lived with great anticipation from meal to meal. Malise also began playing with Petey, giving him a Santa toy so he'd gain confidence.

... Public Response

Petey's picture was posted on the Texas Old English Sheepdog website and Cindy says that the response was astounding. Throughout the U.S. people sent donations to aid Petey's recovery. Because of public generosity, Petey got the best veterinary treatment, food, and supplements. He continued to thrive and by March 1, he was ready for permanent adoption. His hair had grown out and he'd gained considerable weight.

"Our Petey had become a 75lb fluff ball."

Petey was adopted by a lady called Kirsty who drove all the way from Colorado to Texas to collect him. As well as a loving family Peter now has two brothers called Ranger and Abbey.

Iruska

Iruska is a stunning, friendly Alaskan Malamute. When he was ten years old, he was taken by his thoughtless owners to the Animal Shelter in Elko, Nevada. When the owners dumped him off, an employee at the shelter was so upset that she gave them a lecture. "I hope you know that you are condemning this dog to death." The chances of an old dog of this size being adopted were very slim.

... Shelter Procedure

With animals that are picked up as strays, the shelters are required to hold the dog for 3-5 days so that the owners have the opportunity to reclaim a lost pet. In Iruska's case, his owners disowned him and full shelters sometimes have to euthanize the dogs if another shelter will not take them or they are not adopted right away. Fortunately for Iruska, the Elko Shelter contacted Maren Gibson at Arctic Breeds Rescue.

... Nevada to Utah

As with many smaller shelters, Arctic Rescue consists of a small group of volunteers. Maren had no one available to make the 460 mile round trip to Elko and back to Salt Lake City. "The most incredible stories of animal rescue have the common theme of people who really care about the animals literally going the extra mile to save them," says Maren Gibson. An employee of Elko Animal Shelter pulled out all the stops and drove Iruska to the Arctic Breeds Rescue Facility in order to save his life.

... A Good Workout

Malamutes need more exercise than most other breeds otherwise they become bored and look for ways to entertain themselves that can be misconstrued as

"bad behaviour"

Escaping small enclosed spaces was Iruska's favorite hobby – one of the reasons he was dumped in the first place. During Iruska's three weeks at Arctic Breeds Rescue, he went hiking, mountain biking; he got the workout he needed to enable him to relax at night and not get into mischief.

"He did not have any real problems at all. Yes, he's big but is very gentle, completely house trained and does not pull on the leash."

... Networking

Iruska was adopted by a couple referred to Arctic Breeds Rescue by the Alaskan Malamute Assistance League, who were willing to take on a ten year old dog. Iruska is very happy with his new family whether accompanying them horseback riding or crashing out on their couch at night.

Pip

Pip was found walking with a bad limp on a busy street and taken to San Francisco Animal Care and Control in February 2005. The young Chihuahua's front leg had been broken and he had probably been abandoned because of his injury. Clearly Pip had not received any medical care for the break because it was healing improperly.

Pip failed the shelter's temperament test, undoubtedly because he was in such pain. Grateful Dogs Rescue looked beyond the results of the behavior test and decided to rescue Pip rather than allow him to be euthanized. After consulting with several veterinarians, the group opted to try to save the leg – a more expensive surgery than amputation, and a much longer recovery period.

The surgery was successful and the fracture was repaired with a metal plate. Although Pip could have adapted well to life with only three legs, he was now ensured a healthy future with four legs. During the eight weeks of special care required for his recovery, Pip's charming personality began to emerge and his foster parents John and Carla decided to adopt him.

... Pip's Private Jet

This little street dog now has a new career as a co-pilot, flying around California on day trips in John's private plane. He also flies with his guardians to their vacation home in Northern Minnesota in the summer, spending the long warm days boating, swimming, and walking in the woods.

Carla said "Every time I see Pip running to catch a ball or his Floppy Disk, and proudly racing it back to us. I'm so happy that he is running on four strong legs, making the most of the life he almost lost, but for the second chance he got from Grateful Dogs Rescue. People hearing his story always say Pip is a lucky dog and he is, but we are lucky too, because he's our dog."

With his light brown eyes and pinkish-brown nose, Pip was named after the hero of Dickens's Great Expectations. Everyone who knows him has

"Great Expectations" for this little pip of a dog.

Porter

Porter is a two and a half year old tri-coloured Rough Collie rescued in February 2007 by Judy Findley of DCH Animal Adoptions in Sydney. She drove out to Wyong to pick him up from a pound and was devastated by what she saw. Despite being microchipped and registered, when Porter's family were contacted they never came to collect him – he'd been thrown out into the street and left to fend for himself.

… Dreadlocks

His coat was in such a disgusting state that Judy rang the groomers and begged them for help. "He smelt so awful I though I'd be sick several times on the drive back to Sydney." Porter had to have all his fur shaved off, right down to the skin as he had three inch dreadlocks full of flea nests. Despite being bathed and shorn, Judy still picked off a further eighty fleas digging away at his flesh.

Despite the fact Porter had been neglected, he had a lovely sunny nature. He had a bad reaction when he went in to be castrated and had to have his complete scrotum removed because it became so inflamed. "All through this Porter showed an abundance of affection to everyone he met. The vet said he'd never met a nicer boy."

… Melbourne

The Findlays managed to find Porter a lovely family in Melbourne who absolutely worship him. They call him Perfect Porter and you can see from his photo that he is absolutely perfect.

Panda

Panda (short for Pandemonium) was one of ten American Bulldog puppies whose mother had been confiscated by animal control from a drug dealer. The puppies were actually born en route to Jodi Specter's house who works for American Bulldog Rescue. She had offered to try to help animal control find homes for the puppies.

Panda was very ill when he was born and had to be hand fed puppy formula. Panda grew steadily worse and was diagnosed with kidney stones and urinary blockages. Panda has a metabolic disease that stops him breaking down proteins properly.

A lady called Rachael came along to Jodi's house to help her look after the puppies. Rachael fell for the fragile puppy and decided to adopt him.

As if Panda's medical issues were not enough, when he was nine months old, he was also diagnosed with cataracts. Fortunately, his sight has not worsened very much over the last three years and Panda is now a relatively healthy 75lbs lap dog.

... Comedian

Panda has Rachael in fits of laughter as he loves to ham it up – (I mean, just look at that face!) Panda does have typical Bulldog traits – he's very stubborn and set in his ways. If he wants to sleep in, Rachael has a job moving his big bulk off the bed and he often refuses to get out of the car following a visit to the park or beach.

"He is stubborn and a little obnoxious but fits well in our family and we have all grown to love him"

Puzzle

... It Just Takes a Phone Call

One afternoon, the Scottish Society for the Prevention of Cruelty to Animals (SSPCA) received a call that saved poor Puzzle's life. Her story demonstrates just how critical it is to report cruelty immediately. The call came from a woman living in Wester Hailes, a housing estate on the outskirts of Edinburgh. It was to one of these multi-storey flats that the two Scottish SPCA Inspectors were deployed.

Earlier that day, the woman had passed by the front door of an empty flat and had heard a soft scratching noise. When she peered through the letterbox, she felt sure that there was an animal near the door. When the Inspectors arrived, they looked through the letterbox and made out the shape of an animal lying in the dark hallway. A Council Officer was called and they gained entry to the flat.

Photography by Steve Lindridge iDEAL IMAGES

... Barely Breathing

Lying in the hallway was a Dalmatian puppy. She was semi-conscious and whimpered when the Inspector knelt down. She was too weak even to raise her head to acknowledge him. They carried the puppy down the stairs and rushed her to the emergency vets. The vet was horrified at this tiny puppy's condition and was concerned that it was too late to save her. He and his team were determined to give her a fighting chance and started intensive treatment.

... Meanwhile

The Scottish SPCA Inspectors returned to the empty flat to continue their investigation. A stack of mail indicated that the tenants had left around three weeks earlier and the puppy had survived by lapping water from the toilet bowl.

After 49 hours Puzzle's will to live and the excellent treatment from the team of vets allowed the Scottish SPCA to transfer Puzzle to the Society's Lothian Animal Welfare Centre. The staff carefully monitored her progress but noticed that she did not respond to their voices. It was established that the little Dalmation was stone deaf. Day by day she gained strength and six weeks later, the vet examined her and confirmed that she was ready for adoption.

"Laughing Girl"

A few days later, a couple arrived looking to re-home a dog, and spotted (no pun intended) Puzzle. She responded to them immediately and the staff made sure that the couple knew that she would need special care. After the Society checked out the couples' suitability, they took her home. They named her Puzzle and call her their Laughing Girl because she is such a joy. She has been trained using special sign language and during 2003, became a mascot for the Scottish SPCA when they launched their Black and White Spotty Ribbon Appeal.

Sky & Sheena

Krystyna Bell is crazy about her two Border Collies Sky and Sheena. Sky was rescued from Battersea Dogs & Cats Home in July 2006, and Sheena joined their family from the RSPCA on May 12, 2007.

… The Power of a Website

Krystyna and her husband, Gary, did not plan to adopt a dog as they both work all day. They were happy with their two indoor cats, Misia and Maya. However, both of them adore dogs and donate to the RSPCA and sponsor a dog at Dogs Trust. Browsing an RSPCA website, Krystyna came across a heartbreaking story of a dumped Dalmation and decided to make enquiries. However, an experienced dog owner had already pipped Krystyna to the post but unfazed, Krystyna continued to look at the adoption pages on the Dogs Trust and Battersea Dogs & Cats Home websites.

... Sad Dogs

The urge to help one of these sad dogs was overwhelming – Krystyna kept checking the sites for dogs good with cats and eventually, she plucked up the courage to physically visit Battersea Dogs & Cats Home in Windsor.

... The Agony of Choice

Many readers will fully comprehend Krystyna's reticence to actually visit a rescue home's facilities. How do you choose from all those pleading eyes, the wagging tails and "please take me" expressions? On July 22, 2006, Krystyna's birthday, her husband took her to Battersea's Windsor facility to discuss the possibility of adopting a dog bearing in mind that she had not had a dog before and that Battersea prefers to rehome dogs who have had a difficult past to experienced dog owners.

> *"I had to look at Sky because she managed to touch me with her paw; she was desperate to get out of the kennel."*

Thus the choice was made but that was not the end of Krystana's worries. Sky had been brought to Windsor by some people who had thirteen other dogs who had bullied her. She had obviously just had puppies although the people failed to mention this pertinent fact but at least they did not leave her in the street. Most likely, Sky had formerly been abandoned; she was old and had a heart murmur.

... Sky's Heart Murmur

Battersea was completely upfront with Krystyna saying that adopting an older dog (Sky is somewhere between seven and ten years old) with a Grade III heart murmur may not be the best choice for a first adoption. However, Krystyna was determined to give Sky the best years of her life. However, that did not stop her worrying about how long Sky would live. They returned to meet the vet to discuss her heart condition and its implications. Basically, the vet told them that although Sky did not need medication, Sky's remaining years are an unknown quantity and with that knowledge, they took her home to meet the cats.

… 27 July, 2007 and Forward

Although Sky was very unsure of herself to begin with, she has been well behaved and loving from day one. The Bells overcame the problem of them working all day by employing two sympathetic dog walkers and Krystyna now manages to work some days of the week from home. They make sure that even if they are working they walk her at night and spend plenty of time giving her cuddles. "Sky is no trouble and is a pure delight to have around. The only downside is worrying about her health and about losing her, but that is my problem not hers."

… Sheena Arrives

The Bells adopted Sheena, a 6-year-old Border Collie from the RSPCA, Middleborough. She had been tied up all her life and bitten by another dogs. She had deep wounds on her neck from the rope and needed two operations. Very nervous, Sheena was in a foster home for seven months before the Bells came along.

> *"She would only sleep in a crate but after two days she was confident enough to sleep on Sky's bed and never went back inside the crate which has now been removed."*

Although Sheena has gained confidence by being with such loving parents and from Sky, she is still very scared and doesn't trust people. She still refuses to take a treat and twitches at the slightest sound. However, she is affectionate towards the Bells and calls to them when they get up in the morning although she will not go upstairs or wander around the house.

"It is endearing to watch Sheena running about, but sometimes very sad because she looks at times like a prisoner just released who cannot get enough freedom. Both she and Sky eat as if it was their last meal."

Krystyna Ended Her Story By Telling Me This:

"They are both wonderful and I would not be without them. Nothing is too much trouble for me as long as it is for their benefit." If only everyone who owns a dog thought like the Bells.

Skye & Rico

On May 8, 2006, Skye and Rico, two semi-feral German Shepherds, were caught by the local dog warden along with their five- year- old mother, Tessa. They had been seen running wild for some weeks but had managed to avoid capture. They were then brought, in a terrified state, to the Wood Green Animal Shelter in Godmanchester who thought that the young dogs were about eighteen months old. It was clear that they had never had any human contact before – Tessa's background remains unknown but it is likely she was dumped and bought the puppies up scavenging for food and shelter.

> *"Both dogs were thin and Skye had a haematoma in her ear which caused it to flop down, but apart from that they were surprisingly in good health."*

… At Wood Green Shelter

Both dogs were such nervous wrecks that the shelter put them in the shelter's office so that they could get used to being around people. "During this time, Sky would crawl across the floor on her belly to meet people." The shelter used natural flower remedies (Walnut and Larch) to help the dogs relax. However, they continued to be so shy and anxious they would not come out of their kennels for prospective owners to view them. This went on for about a month and Wood Green were concerned that Skye and Rico would never be suitable for re-homing.

On the lead, both dogs hid behind the handler if another dog approached, and although Rico was the braver of the two, it was clear that they could never be separated and would need a home that was prepared to start with the very basics.

... Two Months Later

Finally, two courageous people, seeing the worried looks on the dogs' faces, took the plunge and decided to adopt them. At their new home, Skye continued to be really shy and lay under the table for hours. Their mum and dad spent hours patiently gaining the pairs' trust and it finally paid off.

Tessa, their mum, also had a rough time. She was re-homed on 26th May, returned by the 31st and finally found her forever home on 6th June.

... One Year Later

With time and patient coaxing, she now ventures further afield and has become more confident. They are still unhappy around strangers or other dogs, but social conditioning is bringing results. "They can also be left in the home now without destroying anything although Skye did a bit of wallpaper stripping one day." The two dogs are devoted to each other and it is great to know that there are people like Skye and Rico's parents who are prepared to take on such a "double" challenge.

Tommy

... Track Star

Tommy was born in Ireland on 12th November, 1997. Two years later, he started his racing career in Ireland and England and was quite the track star. He won 8 of his 44 races and placed second in eleven others. Tommy lived in a family home for 2.5 years with a Labrador Bitch. He has come to us as his family have emigrated, leaving him behind.

... Career Over

Tommy's career came to a standstill when he tore a muscle in his back leg in November 2001 and he was sent to Castledon Kennels Greyhound Rescue in search of adoptive parents. 18 months later, he was chosen by a carefully vetted woman with an 8 year old son who adored him and Tommy soon had a companion in the form of a Labrador bitch. Castledon received an email from Tommy's owners everything was just peachy.

… We're Emigrating Without You

In March 2006, Tommy's owner contacted Castledon to say they were emigrating to Australia due to health reasons within the family, but leaving their dogs in the UK. The Labrador was dispatched to another family as a guard dog in a yard. Tommy was sent back to Castledon. Interestingly, Tommy's owner dropped him off at the kennels in March but did not emigrate until the August. Since then, she has never contacted Castledon to see if Tommy, her "beloved" dog had been re-homed.

… Broken Heart

For the first few weeks Tommy seemed OK being back at the kennels – he thought his family were coming back for him. But now more than a year later, he knows that they are not coming back for him and he has become depressed.

> *"He is overlooked because of his age, says Jodie Adams of Castledon Kennels. This is often a problem and there is simply no reason for it. It breaks my heart when I see Greyhounds like Tommy left on the shelf."*

Tommy is a great dog and so very loyal to people he knows. He loves being stroked and will end up leaning against you and almost falling asleep!

Please don't overlook dogs like Tommy because of their age. Don't make them spend the rest of his valiant lives in a kennel. It is very important to remember that old dogs need to find happiness too, they truly deserve it, don't you think?

Jake

… Big Dog; Tiny Flat

Jake is a German Shepherd who was brought to St Francis Animal Welfare when he was two years of age, after his owner could no longer look after him. The owners admitted not exercising Jake which was evident from the underdeveloped state of his legs. He had been kept indoors all day in a small flat and was underweight, filthy and had developed a skin disease called Furonculosis. This is a bacterial condition usually caused by exposure to filthy conditions. It is characterized by recurring boils that eat away healthy tissue. As Jake was suffering from this on his paws, it was agony for him to walk.

… Jake and the Boss

The Chairman of St Francis, Dave Whitmore, was in the reception area when Jake was brought in. Visibly upset, Dave carried Jake down to the kennels himself, where he spent some time with him before carrying on with his kennel duties.

Furonculosis is hard to treat and can require lifelong treatment. Jake underwent six months of intensive treatment, reacted positively to his medication and to his new best friend Dave, who visited him every day. Eventually, his paws healed and he started to grow a proper German Shepherd coat.

Now that Jake was fit and well enough to be adopted, Dave could not bear the thought of being parted from this lovely dog, with whom he had such a bond. It didn't take Dave long therefore, to make the decision to adopt Jake himself. Dave took Jake to agility classes to help his leg muscles to develop and to obedience classes which helped Jake socialise with both dogs and humans.

... Second Chance

Jake is very grateful for his second chance, and is a loyal friend to Dave. He enjoys a happy and spacious home-life with Dave and his family, together with another German Shepherd, Sasha, also a St Francis rescue dog. Jake is able to lead a normal life and has a big garden in which to stretch and relax as well as his several daily walks.

... Tip from Dave

"Jake is an incredibly good natured, affectionate boy – very laid back. I wish people would understand the commitment needed to look after a large dog, and then maybe Jake would not have had to suffer the way he did."

St Francis has a policy of never putting a healthy animal to sleep, and they currently care for several elderly and infirm animals (with treatable conditions), who will probably never find a home. They will be looked after at the shelter for the rest of their lives, unless a suitable owner comes along (see contact details on p. 143).

Victoria

Victoria's story started on the east coast of Scotland in the 'Long Town' of Kirkcaldy. It was a cold mid-December afternoon when two teenage boys returned home after playing football. Their journey took them under the Victoria Railway Bridge and they were shocked to see what looked like the body of a dead dog. As the boys crouched down beside her, the dog opened her eyes and whimpered. One boy ran home to fetch his mother and the other gently covered her with his jacket and spoke quietly to try to reassure the injured dog. The boy's mother rang the Scottish SPCA and she and her son returned to the railway bridge where the three waited anxiously for the Inspector to arrive.

Scottish SPCA Inspectors are trained to investigate animal cruelty as well as rescue animals and the Inspector who examined the dog was suspicious as to how the Staffordshire Bull Terrier had come by her injuries. She appeared to have fallen 100 feet from the bridge, but the fall could not have caused the terrible wound on her left hip.

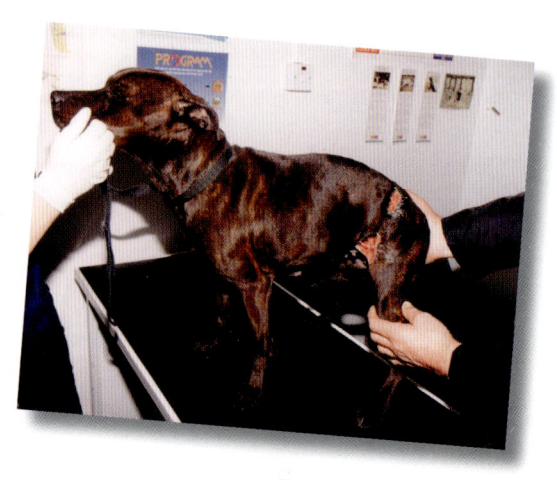

… Unbelievably Cruel

She was rushed to a veterinary surgeon where she was treated for shock and then X-rayed to assess her injuries. The staff had now given the dog a name; Victoria, after the railway bridge where she had been found. Although she was in pain from the fall, she amazingly had no broken bones but it was the wound on her side that was giving cause for concern. Within a few hours, Victoria was able to stand and as the vet looked into the entry of the wound at the top of her hip, he could see through the dog, to the exit wound in her groin. It appeared that Victoria had been skewered!

… Used for Revenge

An appeal for information was made through the local media and the awful truth of Victoria's life became clear. She was owned by a young woman who was in a very violent relationship. She loved her dog very much and her partner used the dog to control his girlfriend. If he was in a bad mood or he perceived she had done something to displease him, he would 'punish' the dog to control her.

Information came to the Society and it was suggested that on the day Victoria was found, her owner had tried to leave her partner. In a terrible rage he had tried to kill the dog with a javelin and his method of disposing of the body was to throw the dog off the Bridge. Amazingly the javelin had missed all her vital organs and she had survived the 100 foot fall.

As the investigation progressed, Victoria's owner had to go into hiding and her partner then threatened to kill the Scottish SPCA Inspector and burn down the Animal Welfare Centre where the dog was now being cared for.

The dog's owner was frightened for her dog's safety and she bravely signed over the ownership of her dog to the Society. This meant that the Scottish SPCA staff could look for a new, safe home for Victoria when she recovered.

As for the man who had harmed Victoria, his threats to the Society suddenly stopped and he disappeared from the area. In spite of extensive enquiries, he was never found and sadly, never prosecuted.

Victoria made an excellent recovery from her physical wounds. The Scottish SPCA Animal Welfare Centre staff now had the job of helping the gentle staffie to learn to trust again.

In Scotland, vet nurses who train together tend to stay in touch with each other and the result is a very powerful network. The vet nurse who initially helped to treat Victoria used the network to help the Scottish SPCA find the perfect home for her. She now lives in the UK with another vet nurse, who has completed Victoria's transformation from terrified dog to happy, loving pet.

Violet

In February 2006 a passerby discovered Violet, an elderly spaniel mix, tied to a tree alongside a busy street. Upon her arrival at San Francisco Animal Care and Control it was immediately apparent that she had multiple medical problems, the most serious being such a very large tumor hanging from her abdomen that made it impossible for her to walk, sit, or lie down comfortably. Because of this condition Violet was scheduled for euthanasia.

Two Grateful Dogs Rescue volunteers happened to spot Violet in the shelter and decided to try to help her so she wouldn't have to spend her last few days in the shelter. The group's veterinarian diagnosed her "tumor" as a huge hernia, the result of many years of neglect. They agreed to try to repair the hernia, a risky procedure with an uncertain outcome, especially given her age and medical condition.

Violet did survive, thanks to the skill of her medical team and the loving care of her foster mom. But her recovery may have been primarily due to Violet herself; that she managed to survive all those years in such deplorable shape was proof of her will to live.

Eleanor and Richard, who have adopted many rescue dogs over the years, fell in love with Violet and decided to adopt her in May 2006. Violet – now renamed Uma – settled in easily with her new family.

> *"It makes me so happy to know that Grateful Dogs Rescue was able to save her life when others would have given up on her."*

Willow

... Too Boisterous

Willow, a male Welsh springer spaniel, was handed over to Springer Spaniel Rescue by a family from Portsmouth because he was too boisterous. Common in springers, he had had trouble with his ears and had one of his inner ears removed. He was re-homed to a family that seemed ideal and whom had been stringently vetted by SSR but two years later, he was back at SSR's kennels due to family problems.

... Transmitting Stress

It was very clear to SSR that the family problems had had a detrimental effect on Willow.

> *"He came to us a very unhappy and sad little boy"*

Like many children, Willow blamed himself for the fights within the family and thought that he was being punished. He could not understand why he kept being shunted off to kennels. Wendy and Glyn Griffiths, directors of SSR worked hard with Willow to boost his confidence. Because of his missing inner ear, he was completely deaf and needed to go to someone who could provide a calm environment and show him masses of love; make him realize that life was worth living.

... Confidence Willow!

Judy Adams took Willow on a trial basis. She was the perfect foster mom and worked with Willow's shyness until he eventually began to gain some self confidence, staking out the front window as his patch. He eventually stopped barking at every passer by, realizing that they had not come to take him away or to threaten Judy. In April 2006, Judy adopted Willow on a permanent basis. Willow has made friends with Thomas, the churchyard cat and now permanent window display in Judy's house. He and Judy won the Doggie of the Year award from SSR – an award given to owners who have adopted particularly difficult dogs.

> **Do's & Don'ts**
> DO be aware that the environment in your home directly affects your pets. Don't take your personal issues out on your animals.

"Won the Doggie of the Year award from SSR – an award given to owners who have adopted particularly difficult dogs.

Winston

Winston was rescued from another shelter by Texas Old English Sheepdog Rescue just as be was about to be put down. He had been dumped at the shelter by his owner who did not even bother to leave a name – his nor the dogs. The shelter thought twice about calling Texas OES because they didn't think Winston had a hope. He had heartworm so badly that he was only a few days from certain death. Chronic coughing indicated that he had congestive heart failure.

"Winston had sores all over his body, his teeth were worn through from chewing his wire cage where he'd been shut up for the last SIX YEARS – all his life"

… Puppy Farm Victim

Texas OES Rescue thought that he was deaf because he showed no reaction whatsoever to any sound and he was so weak that the vet was worried the strength of the heartworm medication would kill him. They also believed that Winston, who was not neutered, had been used for "puppy mill" breeding. His leg muscles had atrophied so badly that he could not walk. Basically, Winston had lost the will to live.

Several days later, Steve Schott of Texas EOS knocked on a window to quieten another dog, and noticed that Winston had looked up, finally reacting to noise. He had obviously been severally traumatized, but that small reaction proved to be a turning point for Winston.

After two months Winston lost his cough and could take several gentle walks a day on Steve's 40 acre wooded property. He was on medication to prevent infection and a raw food diet with supplements to build the immune system. Thanks to donations towards Winston's veterinary bills, Winston survived his slowly administered heartworm treatment (so the dead worms didn't clot the heart and arteries), learned to walk, to run and become a normal dog.

... Distance No Object

Kim and Bob found Winston on the Texas EOS website and flew all the way from Maryland to Texas to meet him. It was love at first sight and they then rented a car to drive Winston 1,450 miles back to Maryland. Steve Schott says that

"Kim and Bob love Winston unconditionally"

and that's essential when you adopt any animal. Winston not only has a happy home, goes to work with his parents, but he even has a Chesapeake Bay beach house for weekends where he chases sand crabs or simply relaxes to the sound of the waves.

Do's & Don'ts

DON'T ever buy a puppy from a puppy farm without contacting the Kennel Club for details of the Accredited Breeder Scheme. This is still not a guarantee that the breeder treats his dogs properly.

Physically go to see the mother with her puppies. NEVER arrange to meet a dealer at some other location. If you feel suspicious, don't patronize the dealer and call your local rescue shelter immediately.

"Please consider being a much-appreciated hero to an animal in need. The rewards are as innumerable as they are priceless."

Belle

Belle is another dog rescued by Tamera Gibson of Animal Aid, Inc in Florida. She is a black Chihuahua mix who was kept chained in the Florida heat by her family. She was very thin and lay panting in the dirt trying to wriggle her way into a cool patch.

Tamera approached Belle who, even in her dehydrated state, raised her head to acknowledge Tamera's voice. Tamera knocked on the door to speak to Belle's family about leaving her outside without shade. Her callous owner made it abundantly clear that he'd be thrilled to "unload" Belle and that Tamera could "take his burden."

Tamera bought Belle back to her shelter, bathed her, treated her for skin infections, and gave her a square meal. After one month's recovery at the shelter, Belle met Beth and Belle shot the proverbial Cupid's arrow straight through Beth's heart. The two live for each other and Belle is glued to Beth's side. Belle now lives inside and has a bed to sleep in and a special diet to keep her healthy.

… A Last Word from Tamera

> *"Happy ever after does not only occur in fairy tales; it happens in animal shelters where caring people come together to rescue a dog in need. Belle's story epitomizes the essence of rescue."*

Yunku

... Dog Aid and KAPS

The story of Yunku is disturbing to say the least, but I feel that it should be told in order to make the public more aware of the atrocities taking place in South Korea. Her story involves two rescue societies – DogAid founded in 2001 based in Victoria, Australia and the Korean Animal Protection Society (KAPS) founded by Sunnan Kum. DogAid is the sole Australian representative for KAPS. They promote the plight of animals in South Korea by trying to get the Australian public to sponsor Korean animals and to write protest letters to South Korean politicians to get laws changed. There is no reason that readers from other countries cannot send donations directly to KAPS (see contact details on p. 142). The situation in South Korea is desperate – read on....

Miss Yunhee is an employee for a company located in Pahodong, Dalseaogu, Daegu. She started feeding a feral mongrel who would creep into the company's garden scavenging for food. About a month later, the dog failed to show up and kindhearted Miss Yunhee was worried.

A few days later the dog dragged itself back to the garden but Miss Yunhee realized that its situation had become even worse. She found horrific injuries on the vertex and someone must have viciously beaten the dog as there were two large holes in its head and the skull was exposed. Miss Yunhee tried to catch the dog but it was too scared. After three days, the holes were full of maggots. Miss Yunhee called Sunnan Kum at KAPS who managed to catch the poor animal and take it to Beside Museum Animal Hospital.

… Vet Lim

The mongrel, now named Yunku, would allow no one near her but fortunately, she was in the capable hands of veterinarian Lim who managed to anesthetize her. "From head, to mouth, to eyes, there was no square inch left undamaged." Thanks to continuous shots and oral meds for ten days, Yunku's open wounds began to granulate. She also received regular meals for the first time in her life and allowed people to look at her face and take photos. Once she has become stable, Yunku will be moved to the Boeun Shelter for adoption.

… Dog Traders in South Korea

It turned out that Yunku had escaped from a dog trader. Dog traders capture stray dogs, hang them from a tree, and then sell the bodies for meat. Sunnan Kum supposes that Yunku put up a fight as her head wounds looked as if she'd been beaten by a hammer.

> *"Butchers continue to promote meat from tortured dogs to be a sexual stimulant and a cure for the summer heat"*

Jack

... September 11th – Casualty of Cruelty

Jack, an eight-year-old Irish Terrier, was saved from certain death by Limerick Animal Welfare. Jack had virtually no body fat and was almost bald because he was suffering from starvation and Sarcoptes mange. Limerick Animal Welfare did not think he would live. His life before he was bought to the shelter is unknown. You can see from the photos that it can only have been horrendous.

... Chronic Illness

Limerick knew that Jack had been in this appalling state for a long time because his skin had thickened in a desperate attempt to protect him from the elements as he had no fur. He scratched non-stop and was started on emergency veterinary treatment. Despite his extreme condition Jack was affectionate and understandably relished mealtimes.

... Fabulous Foster Mum

On September 14, after two days in hospital, Jack arrived at his foster home. He was still terribly weak and although everything was being done for him, Limerick and his foster mum had to play a waiting game to see if he'd pull through. He slept most of the time and ate several small meals a day.

"Jack gave his foster mum "the paw" and even had the strength to bark."

… September 19th

Four days after arriving at his foster home, Jack turned the corner. His black, ravaged skin began to shed, he ate well and he stopped scratching quite so much. As his energy increased, he finally had the strength to bark.

… Different Dog

By the 24th September, a different Jack began to emerge. He loved his foster home and its surrounding countryside and was able to go for a short walk.

"We were so touched how much love Jack showed us…it was hard for us to understand Jack's ability to forgive and how quickly he learned to trust."

October 16th

A red-letter day for Jack! His adoptive mum Janet came for the first time to visit him, flying from England. Janet could only visit as Jack was not yet ready to travel but on October 29th, Jack accompanied Janet and husband Martin home to their house in the country.
"This morning he is full of beans and very quizzy; into everything. I thought he might be a bit subdued after so long a journey and so many faces – but not a bit of it."

… Jack Becomes a Teddy

Jack continues to thrive in his loving new home, has gained weight and a ton of fur. Janet and Martin decided to re-name him Teddy – the name Jack would always have an association with his former destitute life. Indeed, the photos show a radically changed dog. Isn't he fabulous.

Tiny Tim

Tamera Gibson, Managing Director of Animal Aid, Inc in Florida, has some great rescue stories.

> *"I know rescue will always be my life and every dog saved and placed makes the tears all worthwhile"*

Tiny Tim a pocket sized sweetheart not only brought tears to Tamera's eyes but "my heart did not just break it wrenched."

… Horrendous Decision

Tamera discovered Tiny Tim at the Miami/Dade. Animal Control. She is a regular visitor at the public shelter, forced, like other private rescue groups, to make the horrendous decision which animals to kill and which to save. She clearly hates this part of her job. "My heart wavers over every dog that looks back at me with a forlornness that only a caged animal can give."

When she saw Tiny Tim with his eye just removed by Miami Services and his front leg dangling helplessly, she knew she'd take him but was concerned with what the future costs would be for his special needs and ongoing treatment. Her shelter was at full capacity and Tamera specializes in animals that need special attention in order for them to be placed.

> *"I reached my arms out to hold him and stroked his head. I felt his tongue on my tears.*
> *'It will be OK,'*
> *he seemed to whisper."*

… Praying for Donations

Tamera left with Tiny Tim that same day wondering if she'd lost her mind. She says he kept his eye on her the whole drive back to Bayview Animal Hospital where he had surgery. Tiny Tim had to have his smashed leg amputated where he had more than likely been hit by a car.

Tamera posted his story on Animal Aid's website and prayed for donations. Within a week, donations had enabled Tamera to take Tiny Tim.

… A One Eyed, Three Legged Dog

Tamera kept updating her website telling Tiny Tim's story hoping that once he had recovered, some kind person would take on the challenge of a one eyed, three legged dog. Dan and Jennifer rose to the challenge; in fact they could not wait to add Tiny Tim to their family.

> *"Tiny Tim is now known as Chop-Chop and is doing just fine."*

Pansy

Pansy was only seven weeks old when she was bought along with two other puppies to Dorset Animal Workers Group rescue home. This no kill policy rescue society keeps animals in their own homes until suitable homes can be found. Because of the incredible number of abandoned animals, life as a rescuer is never easy.

"One Christmas I had twenty-six dogs living in our terraced house and all my foster homes were full."

… Let's Play Football – With Puppies

The puppies were being used by a group of children as footballs. It is impossible to imagine that children can be this cruel and thoughtless but it happens more frequently that you would think. A member of the public reported the situation and the puppies were rescued by Helen Griffiths and some of her volunteers for Dorset Animal Workers Group.

… Broken Ribs

All three puppies were emaciated, had mange and pot bellies from worms. They also had broken ribs from being kicked about. The vet treated their injuries and very slowly began worming them – slowly because if puppies are wormed too quickly when full of parasites, they can die. Any noise or quick movement caused the puppies to scream with fear and it took several days before they were brave enough to eat from a bowl.

… Only One Survives

Tragically, the toll on the health of two of the puppies proved too much for their tiny systems and they died. Helen and her helpers were devastated. Pansy however, pulled through and was taken under the wing of an American Bulldog cross called Staffy, who was also housed at Helen's house. Pansy would curl up with him at night while he cleaned her.

... Home at Last

Pansy was eventually adopted by a lovely retired couple from Poole who have since returned to Dorset Animal Workers Group to adopt a companion for her.

> **Do's & Don'ts**
> Do leave the radio or TV on if you are out – familiar noise is mental company for your dog. However, this is not an alternative to human contact.

Heather

"A greyhound had been found collapsed in a field in County Kerry." This was the message received by Amanda Saunders Perkins of Kerry Greyhound Connection who runs a small greyhound rescue and re-homing programme.

The greyhound had in fact collapsed from loss of blood because her ears had been barbarically severed. Naturally, she was in agony and the man who found her and made the call rushed her to the vet. She was treated for severe shock and her open wounds were stitched to stem the flow of blood.

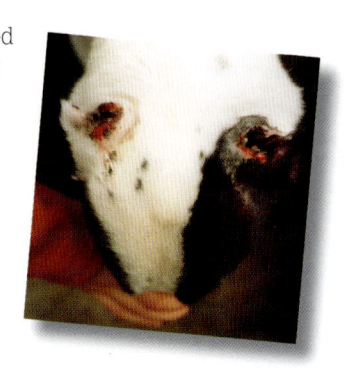

Bureaucracy

Amanda drove straight to the vets but was told that as she was a stray, she had to spend five obligatory days in the local pound to see if she was claimed. Amanda was livid. "Five days in the dog pound when she had suffered cruelty of the highest order not to mention surgery." As Greyhounds are tattooed inside their ears, Heather's owner had obviously wanted to get rid of evidence of ownership by hacking off her ears. He'd obviously left her for dead in the field, secure that he could not be traced.

At dawn five days later Amanda was at the Pound's doorstep. Needless to day, no one had claimed her. "I was the only person who wanted a sad little Greyhound bitch with no ears. She walked quietly up to me and put her sweet face right up to mine."

Heather, as she was now called got into Amanda's car all set to go to the kennels where she'd be living until a home could be found. But somehow, Amanda's foot seemed rooted to the gas pedal and she drove right past and took her home. "I made her up a comfy bed by the radiator. I already had five hounds at home so I could only keep her until her poor ears healed." Amanda enlisted the help of Greyhound Rescue of West England to find Heather a special, permanent home.

Wobbly

Heather's confidence increased but because her inner ears were exposed to the elements, she would lose her balance when out walking in windy weather. Once the raw areas around the ears healed, Amanda put a scarf around Heather's head to keep the weather out.

Spokesdog

Heather was adopted by a great lady called Rona. Heather and Rona go to Cruft's Dog Show every year to tell people about the unscrupulous side to Greyhound racing. Amanda and her daughter also go to Cruft's and get a great welcome from Heather. Thanks to Kerry Greyhound Connection, Heather has a reason to wag her tail.

List of Dog Rescue Homes

American Bulldog Rescue (Panda)
Offices throughout the USA
www.americanbulldogrescue.com
Newtown, PA
Email: jodi.specter@verizon.net

Animal Aid, Inc (Tiny Tim & Belle)
Attn: Tamera Gibson
2121 W Oakland Park Blvd. Suite 6,
Oakland Park,
Fort Lauderdale, FL 33311
Tel: (954) 730-8398
Email: tamerac@aol.com
www.animal-aid.com

Animals In Need Maxicare (Murray)
P.O. Box 145
Northampton NN1 3AQ
Tel: 01604-636323
Email: animals-in-need@maxicare.
  freeserve.co.uk
www.animals-in-need.org.uk

Animal Savers California (Burlap)
Sacramento, CA
Email: animalsaverscal@yahoo.com
www.geocities.com/
  animalsaversofcalifornia

Arctic Breeds Rescue
159 West 500 North
Provo, UT 84601
Tel: (801) 318-0155
Email: maren@arcticrescue.com
www.arcticrescue.org

Battersea Dogs & Cats Home
4 Battersea Park Rd
Battersea
London SW8 4AA
Tel: (020) 7622-3626

Also at: Old Windsor
Priest Hill
Old Windsor
Berkshire SL4 2JN
Tel: 01784- 432929

And at: Brands Hatch
Crowhurst Lane
Ash
Kent TN15 7HH
Tel: 01474- 874994
www.dogshome.org
Email: info@dogshome.org

Boxer Angels Rescue, Inc. (Humphrey)
PO Box 543
N. Bellmore, NY 11710
Tel: 1-877-598-7752
Email: boxerangelsdirectors@yahoo.com
www.boxerangelsrescue.com

BullsEye Dog Rescue (Clyde)
P.O. Box 28172
Seattle, WA
Email: info@bullseyerescue.org
www.bullseyerescue.org
www.maxtheshelterdog.com/kidsforpits.
  html
www.badrap.org/rescue/index.cfm
pbrc.net/

Canine Connections (Buddy)
33010 SE 99th
Snoqualmie, WA 98065
Tel: (425) 831-2578
Email: simpsmj@dhs.wa.gov
www.k9connections.org

Castledon Kennels Greyhound Rescue
Jodie Adams (Tommy)
181 Castledon Road
Wickford
Essex SS12 0EG
Tel: 01268 733293
Email: info@grehoundrescue.co.uk
www.greyhoundrescueukco.uk

Ceredigion Animal Rescue & Education
Llwynderw Fawr
Llanarth
Ceredigion SA47 0PU
Wales
Phone: (0845) 310 5663
Email:contact@ceredigionanimalrescue.
    org.uk
www.ceredigionanimalrescue.org.uk

DABS (The Domestic Animal Birth-control Society)
PO Box 73
Canterbury, NSW, 2193, Australia
Tel: (02) 9798 6767
http://www.dabs.org.au/index.html

DCH Animal Adoptions
Judy & Robert Findlay (Kane)
Collie Rough Foster Carers
Email: dchanimaladoptions@iprimus.
    com.au
http://home.iprimus.com.au
Sydney Australia (02) 9674 4824
www.dchanimaladoptions.com.au

DogAid Australia
P.O. 6050 Karingal,
Victoria 3199
Email: dogaid@hotmail.com
www.dogaid.freeservers.com

Dorset Animal Workers Group (Pansy, Yoda)
Tel:01202 380467 or 01202 428868
Email: helengriffiths2110@hotmail.co.uk
www.dawgdogs.co.uk

Farplace Animal Rescue (Meg, 9 puppies)
Sidehead Westgate
Co Durham
DL13 1LE
Telephone: 01388 517397
Mobile: 07860 523434
Email: jan@farplace.co.uk
www.farplace.co.uk

Hope Rescue (Laddie)
Donations: C.Donaghue
14 Heol Eglwys,
Coelbren,
Neath,
SA10 9PF
Tel: 07870 529650
Email: dogs@hoperescue.org.uk
www.hoperescue.org.uk

German Shepherd Rescue (Heidi)
Birchgrove
Castleton Rd
Auchterarder,
Perthshire
PH3 1JW
Email: info@germanshepherdrescue.co.uk
www.germanshepherdrescue.co.uk

Grateful Dogs Rescue (Pip, Violet and Lex)
P.O. Box 411013
San Francisco, CA 94141
Tel: (415) 587-1121
Email: info@gratefuldogsrescue.org
www.gratefuldogsrescue.org

Greek Animal Rescue (Mazzel)
69 Great North Way,
Hendon, London NW4 1PT
Email: info@greekanimalrescue.com
www.greekanimalrescue.com

Hopalong Animal Rescue
P.O. Box 27507
Oakland, CA 94602
(510) 267-1915 tel.
(510) 444-3741 fax
Email: info@hopalong.org
www.hopalong.org

Phil and Deanna Cuchiaro
Irish Setter Rescue New Jersey
34 Ridge Road
Whitehouse Station, NJ 08889
Tel: (732)514-6014
Email: irishrescue1@aol.com
www.irishrescue.org

Sunnan Kum – KAPS (In association with DogAid) (Yunko)
1593-19 Daemyoung-10dong,
Nam-Gu
Daegu City,
South Korea 705-815
Tel: 82-53-622-3588.
Fax: 82-53-656-3587
www.koreananimals.org.kr
*Please see website regarding donations.

The Labrador Lifeline Trust (Jenny, Daisy, Esther)
www.labrador-lifeline.co.uk
Email: selabres@btconnect.com
See website for contact address – TLLT have offices throughout the UK.

Limerick Animal Welfare
59 Parnell St,
Limerick. (Donations)
Tel: 061 336740 087 6371044
email queries@limerickanimalwelfare.com
www.limerickanimalwelfare.com

London Shelter
601 Lordship Lane
Wood Green
London
N22 5LG
Tel: 08701 90 44 40
http://www.woodgreen.org.uk

McKamey Animal Care and Adoption Center (Harry)
c/o Animal Care Trust
P.O. Box 1028
Hixson, TN 37343
Tel: (423) 425-3750
Email: donna@mckameyanimalcenter.org
www.mckameyanimalcenter.org

Mme R. Meinel (Bella)
22 Rue Cassan
34530 Montagnac
France.
04 67 24 09 70
Please note: M. Meinel died during the writing of this book so Madame Meinel needs all the support she can get to keep her kennels open.

Northern California Sled Dog Rescue (NORSLED) (Matsi)
P.O. Box 5784
Vallejo, CA 94591
Tel: 1-800-471-5822
Email: rescue@norsled.org
www.norsled.org

Operation Kindness
3201 Earhart Drive
Carrollton, TX 75006
Tel L 972) 418-PAWS
Email: ok@operationkindness.org
www.operationkindness.org

June Bird
SAY NO TO ANIMALS IN PET SHOPS INCORPORATED
PO Box 799
Bowral
NSW 2576
Australia
www.saynotoanimalsinpetshops.com
Email: icon@binternet.com.au

St. Francis Animal Welfare (Fran & Jake)
Sunnyside Cottage,
Mortimer's Lane, Fair Oak,
Hampshire, SO50 7EA,
United Kingdom
Tel: 023 80 693282
Email: info@sfaw.co.uk
www.sfaw.co.uk"

Scottish SPCA (Puzzle & Vctoria)
Braehead Mains
603 Queensferry Road
Edinburgh
EH4 6EA
Tel (0131) 339-0222
Email: enquiries@scottishspca.org
www.scottishspca.org

Second Chance Animal Rescue (Hilda)
P.O. Box 2958
San Rafael, CA 94912
(415) 506-0161 tel.
(415) 506-0345 fax
Email: info@secondchancerescue.com
www.hopalong.org

Glyn & Wendy Griffiths at **Springer Spaniel Rescue** (Baggins, Jake, Willow)
18 Mill Lane, Parbold,
Lancs, WN8 7NW,
Tel: 01257 464130
http://springerrescue.org.uk/
info@springerrescue.org.uk

Texas Old English Sheepdog Rescue, Inc.
P.O. Box 667053
Houston, Texas 77266-7035
http://www.texasoesrescue.org
texasoesrescue@hotmail.com

The Stubbington Ark Animal Shelter (Max)
In assoc. With RSPCA Solent
174-176 Ranvilles Lane
Stubbington
Fareham
Hants
PO14 3EZ
Tel: 01329-666918
www.stubbingtonark.org.uk

Von Barber
Victorian Canine Rescue
Melbourne, Victoria, Australia 3984
Tel: 0401-034-800
Email: vonchalm@bigpond.net.au
www.victoriancaninerescue.org

Walkin' The Bark Rescue (Iris)
4464 Lone Tree Way #1064
Antioch, CA 94531
Email: dogs@walkinthebark.org
www.WalkinTheBark.org

Wood Green Animal Shelters (Bambi, Leo/Oscar, Sky/Rico)
Email: info@woodgreen.org.uk
www.woodgreen.org.uk

... the last word

Writing the Dog Rescue Book has been a fulfilling and rewarding experience. I say "writing" but it is really the contributors that are the writers – they have been amazing, and some big societies such as the Battersea Cats & Dogs Home the Scottish SPCA, and other smaller private rescues like Grateful Dogs Rescue in San Francisco, have contributed several stories.

Although many of the stories are traumatic, I hope with all my heart that this book makes people either donate, foster and/or adopt. The book is also geared to educate the public as to what to expect and how much time and effort is involved having any pet. Most of the stories in the book have "happy endings" but we must never become complacent. There are literally millions of abandoned, suffering animals that need a kind home. So, to my readers, don't just gloss over the pages, please take action."

Louisa Adams has a B.A. in Liberal Arts from Sonoma State University and an M.F.A from National University in San Diego. She now lives in France with her 5 rescue cats.

Photographed by Gloria Parke

Louisa with "Cleo", the publisher's dog rescued from County Wicklow, Eire over 10 years ago. She was our inspiration for this book!